Gwen Marston

Lively Little
FOLK-ART QUILTS

20 Traditional Projects to Piece & Appliqué

C&T PUBLISHING

Text © 2006 Gwen Marston

Artwork © 2006 C&T Publishing, Inc.

Publisher: Amy Marson

Editorial Director: Gailen Runge

Acquisitions Editor: Jan Grigsby

Editor: Darra Williamson

Technical Editors: Elin Thomas and Georgie Gerl

Copyeditor/Proofreader: Wordfirm, Inc.

Cover Designer: Kristen Yenche

Design Director/Book Designer: Rose Wright

Illustrator: Tim Manibusan

Production Assistant: Kiera Lofgreen

Photography: Luke Mulks unless otherwise noted. Author photo by Harry Littell Photography.

Published by C&T Publishing, Inc., P.O. Box 1456, Lafayette, CA 94549

Front cover: *Floral Bouquet in Batiks* by Gwen Marston

Back cover: *Four-Patch With Streak o' Lightning* and *Puppies*, both by Gwen Marston

Dedication

In memory of my friend Judy Hester, who made the quilt *Aunt Anne's South Carolina Lily* (page 64) as a gift for me. Judy took the pattern from a family quilt and named it after its maker. Judy was a hand piecer and hand quilter, and she did both with great style and expertise.

Acknowledgments

As quiltmaking is primarily a woman's art form, I have always felt honored to be a part of this long tradition. First teachers often make a lasting impression. My first teachers were a group of Mennonite women, followed by Mary Schafer, the great Michigan quiltmaker. I remember the selflessness of these women, who were all about giving and sharing what they knew about quiltmaking. I would like to acknowledge their generosity and the generosity of other quilter friends who have enriched my life and set such a noble example. I also thank my editor, Darra Williamson, for her advice and support throughout the writing of this book. I thank my publisher, C&T Publishing, as well.

Library of Congress Cataloging-in-Publication Data

Marston, Gwen.

 Lively little folk-art quilts : 20 traditional projects to piece & appliqué / Gwen Marston.

  p. cm.

 Includes bibliographical references.

 ISBN-13: 978-1-57120-357-1 (paper trade)

 ISBN-10: 1-57120-357-5 (paper trade)

 1. Patchwork--Patterns. 2. Quilting--Patterns. 3. Appliqué--Patterns. 4. Miniature quilts. I. Title.

 TT835.M27248 2006

 746.46'041--dc22   2005029855

Printed in China

10 9 8 7 6 5 4 3 2 1

Contents

Introduction

I first began to take small quilts seriously when Thomas K. Woodward and Blanche Greenstein published Crib Quilts and Other Small Wonders (see the Bibliography on page 79). Until that time, I made only bed-size quilts, and I used to be kinda smug about it, too. I thought anyone who made small quilts just didn't know any better, or was just plain lazy. This view was fostered by my own ignorance, and the Woodward/Greenstein book woke me up to the fact that small quilts had been around for a long time and had a special place in the history of American quiltmaking.

So I started making doll quilts. I made the first one with leftovers from a full-size quilt, and I now have over 400 little quilts. I've had seven museum showings of small quilts and find that these little beauties lend themselves perfectly to successful exhibits. Because of their size, I am able to show more quilts, and it's possible to include something to please everyone.

My early efforts in working on a small scale focused on exploring traditional patterns. As a young quilter, I admired many traditional quilts, but I knew it wasn't likely I'd have time to make them all as full-size bed quilts. By working small, I was able to investigate many of the patterns that intrigued me. From the beginning, I found making small quilts both delightful and satisfying. I was soon to discover many other advantages to making small quilts. Now, looking back, I feel that making small quilts, more than any other single factor, helped me develop my quiltmaking skills and my understanding of aesthetics.

Now, looking back, I feel that making small quilts, more than any other single factor, helped me develop my quiltmaking skills and aesthetics.

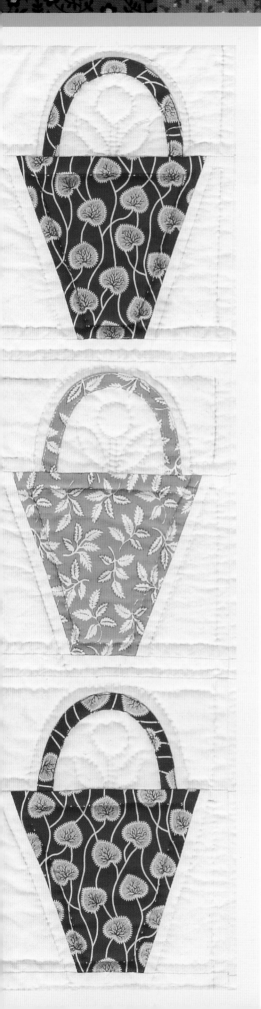

Here are some of the reasons why:

- When "working small," I found that I could experiment with many more ideas and that I was more adventuresome. Making small quilts took me to places I don't think I would have ventured otherwise. I experimented with different techniques, different fabrics, and original designs. Making a small quilt carried less risk, in terms of both time and expense. Therefore, I found myself willing to try anything and everything.

- I worked in a series for the first time. Working small made that possible in a way that wasn't feasible when I was making large quilts and hand quilting them. I have eclectic taste when it comes to quilts, so I was unsuccessful in sticking to one style long enough to create a series until I discovered the small-quilt format.

- Small quilts make great gifts.

- Small quilts have long kept dollies warm. You may know someone special who needs a doll quilt.

- Small quilts make wonderful teaching aids. I can show many more samples in my classes. They are easy to pack when I travel … and easy to store at home.

- Small quilts are wonderful for beginning and advanced quilters alike. Beginners can learn and master the necessary techniques by working small as well as large. Advanced quilters can experiment quickly with new ideas.

- Small quilts are quick and easy and just plain fun …

- … and you can actually get them done!

- Finally, sometimes it can be very healing just *to sew,* and to sew something simple—times when big, complicated projects are simply not appealing. Sometimes, I just need to sit at my sewing machine and make a bunch of Four-Patch blocks and sew them together into a little quilt. I do this just for myself, because it makes me feel better!

I welcome you to the wonderful world of small quilts. Jump right in, and it won't be long before you have a collection of your own. My friend Mary Schafer said it best: "Making doll quilts is just like eating candy." She was right. They are a joy to make.

Appliqué Basics

Many of the quilts in this book include appliqué. Appliqué is a French word meaning "applied." It is nothing more than sewing one piece of fabric onto another. In earlier times, patches were simply laid on the ground, needle-turned under, and stitched, and that was that. I use these traditional techniques because I want to achieve effects similar to those I see repeatedly in older quilts.

"Back-to-basics" appliqué is easy. You simply sew one piece of cloth onto another. It does not require any special tools. You can do it with your basic sewing kit: needles, pins, thread, scissors, and ruler. You just cut out the patches, baste them on the ground with large stitches to hold them in place, and needle-turn the edges under.

Assembling the Tools

Having the *right* tool for the job is important. Having *quality* tools is also important. I still make my quilts using only a few tools. The only new quilting tools I have added are a rotary cutter, a mat, and a collection of Omnigrid rulers.

Scissors: You'll need a good pair of sharp scissors for cutting fabric. For appliqué, I use a tiny pair of 4-inch-long, sharp-pointed scissors.

Pins and Needles: I prefer fine silk pins for any piecing or appliqué project. Silk pins are thin and slip into the fabric easily without pulling or puckering the cloth.

I learned to quilt with a size 9 quilting needle (also called a *Between*) and still use one for all of my sewing tasks. Experiment with different needles to see which one works best for you. Keep in mind that the larger the number, the smaller the needle. In other words, a size 10 needle is smaller than a size 9 needle. Whatever size you choose, make sure it has an eye large enough to see for threading.

Thread: I use 100% cotton thread for hand appliqué. Cotton is easier to thread through the eye of the needle, is less likely to fray at the ends, and won't tangle or knot as easily as cotton-wrapped polyester thread.

Mettler embroidery thread is my favorite for appliqué, with the Mettler silk-finish variety my second choice. For hand quilting, I like thread with a glazed finish. The finish makes threading the needle easier, keeps the thread from knotting, and gives the thread strength.

Templates: All my appliqué quilts in this book were made either with paper templates or without any templates at all, much as they would have been made in the nineteenth century. (See page 7 for more on my cutting methods.)

If you prefer, you can trace the patterns that accompany each appliqué project and make exact templates from a material that will hold its shape and size.

I frequently use two tones of the same color in my quilts. For example, I might choose two reds that are just different enough in tone to add depth and interest to the quilt.

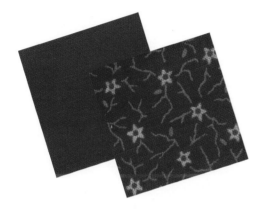

Cutting shape from fabric with ³/₁₆″ seam allowance included in paper template

Adding ³/₁₆″ seam allowance when cutting shape from fabric

Choosing Fabric

For appliqué projects, good-quality, 100% cotton fabrics are—hands down—the wisest choice. They are easier to work with than polyester blends because they hold a crisp, firm crease for turned edges. Look for cottons with a smooth feel and a close, even weave.

When I am working in the folk-art style, I look at antique folk-art quilts—the colors they include and the way those colors are combined. Nowadays, we have an amazing array of fabrics from which to choose, including reproduction prints from the nineteenth century up through the 1930s.

I rely heavily on my intuition when selecting colors and prints for my quilts. I go to my fabric collection and pull out fabrics that I think might work. Then I place them on the floor next to one another, study them, and try to refine my selections. Often, I choose enough fabrics to get started and then add others as the quilt progresses.

Preparing the Fabric

I think it is best to wash fabrics before putting them into a quilt, especially when I'm using strong colors. I want to make sure the fabrics are colorfast and also to remove the sizing, which softens the fabric and makes it easier to hand quilt. I typically wash my fabric in warm water using a mild detergent and then dry it in the dryer or over the line.

Cutting the Shapes

To use the appliqué patterns provided, draw around an accurately traced, finished-size template on the right side of the fabric, and then cut ³/₁₆ inch beyond the pencil line to add the seam allowance. As you stitch the patches to the ground, you will use the pencil line as a guide for turning under the raw edges of the appliqué shape.

If you are feeling more adventurous, you may prefer to pass up the printed patterns in the book and cut the patterns from paper, as I do. Cut a sheet of plain paper the size of the block, sketch the design on the paper, and refine or modify the drawing as needed. Cut out the paper shapes. (You can add the ³/₁₆-inch seam allowances now or when you cut out the fabric pieces.) Pin the patterns on the fabric as you would a commercial dress pattern, and then cut out the fabric pieces. If you need multiples of the same shape, you can layer the fabric and cut four layers at a time.

Once you've experimented with paper, it is an easy leap to cutting shapes directly from fabric. Draw the shapes right onto the wrong side of the fabric so you can change any lines you wish. You can add the seam allowance to the drawn shape, or draw the shape the exact size and add the seam allowance when you cut out the fabric piece.

Placing the Appliqué Patches

The method you use to position appliqués on the ground affects the look of your finished quilt. Some methods result in consistent placement, while others result in varying degrees of inconsistency.

Free-Placement Method: Our eyes can measure distances much more precisely than we think. Also conveniently close at hand—and ideal for measuring short distances—are our fingers. When I am placing appliqués on the ground, I use my thumb and index finger to measure the distance between the shapes and the distance from a patch to the edge of the block. I want some variation in the placement of the pieces, and placing them by eye and hand gives me the nineteenth-century look I am after.

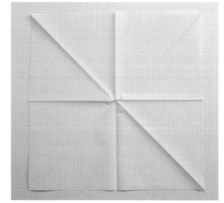

Free-Placement Method

Fold the Ground for Guidelines Method: Fold the ground block in half, top to bottom and side to side, and then on the diagonal in both directions. Use the fold lines to center and determine placement of the appliqué pieces.

The Mary Schafer Method: Mary Schafer, the great Michigan quilter, has a precise method for placement that is a big improvement over tracing the entire design. She places the pattern under the ground and puts a tiny, light pencil dot to indicate where the patches begin and end. A dot at the stem and another dot at the end of a leaf are guide enough for Mary to place each leaf in its exact position.

Fold the Ground for Guidelines Method

Technique

Simply stated, my method for making appliqué quilts is to add the shapes one at a time, baste them on the ground with large stitches just to hold them in place, and then needle-turn and stitch the edges under. Here are my tips for making your appliqué go smoothly:

- Always work in good light.
- Use 100% cotton fabric for both appliqué patches and ground.
- Use 100% cotton thread that matches the appliqué patch.
- Use a needle that is comfortable in your hand.

Mary Schafer Method

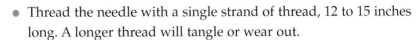

1

2

- Thread the needle with a single strand of thread, 12 to 15 inches long. A longer thread will tangle or wear out.

- Work on a flat surface, such as your leg or a magazine, to stabilize the work. Do not hold the work in midair and try to sew!

- Baste with large stitches to hold the patch in position. Thread basting keeps large pieces from slipping and ensures that you don't work in fullness behind the patch. For small patches, I often pin baste.

- Start with a knot under the appliqué patch, instead of on the back of the ground. This is especially important when you are sewing with dark thread on a white ground, as the thread tail may show through the top.

- If you are right-handed, work from right to left. Reverse if you are left-handed. Keep the edge you are stitching parallel to yourself.

- Clip inside curves with a good brand of small, sharp-pointed scissors, but *only* if you need to and not until you get close to the curve.

- Reinforce inside curves with two or three stitches.

- Don't clip outside curves.

- End by tying a knot on the back of the ground. Then slip the needle between the two layers toward the middle of the patch and snip the thread. This keeps the tail end of the thread from showing through the top.

- Lightly press your work when you are done.

Needle-Turn Appliqué

Needle-turn refers to a method of using the needle to turn under the edges of an appliqué shape as you stitch. Using thread that matches the patch makes the stitches less visible.

1. Hide the knot under the appliqué patch and bring the needle out at the turned-under edge of the patch.

2. Continue to turn the edge of the fabric under by slipping the needle under the appliqué fabric and running the needle along at an angle. Turn under tight curves about ¼″ to ½″ ahead as you sew, and turn under long, straight edges about 1″ ahead.

3. Insert the needle back into the ground fabric exactly beside or slightly behind the exit point and slightly under the lip (or the edge) of the patch. The stitch should be a bit smaller than ⅛″.

4. Bring the needle up again, catching 2 or 3 threads on the very edge of the patch. If your needle catches too much of either the ground or the patch, the stitches are more likely to be visible. Make the stitch with one movement, keeping the stitch as tiny as possible.

4

5. Pull the stitch through snugly, but not so tight that the appliqué patch puckers and won't lie flat.

Handling Inside Curves

Clip inside curves when you are about 1″ to 2″ away if necessary to make them turn smoothly. If you clip all the inside curves on a patch at once, the edges are more likely to ravel.

1. Using small, sharp scissors, clip about ⅛″ into the seam allowance at the curve.

2. Roll under the edges of the patch with the side of your needle and reinforce the clipped curve with 2 or 3 stitches. Take a little bigger bite of the appliqué patch than usual to make sure the inside curve is stable and won't fray.

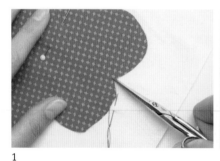
1

2

Cutting out the ground behind an appliqué patch is a relatively new technique; I choose not to do it. I think cutting out the ground behind the appliqué patches makes the quilt less stable, and I don't have trouble quilting through the extra layer of fabric. Cutting away the ground is also a time-consuming step that I am happy to eliminate.

I do cut away patches if they are layered—for example, when I am stitching a smaller flower in the center of a larger flower. In this case, I sew the small flower onto the large flower and then cut away the fabric behind the small flower before I appliqué the large, layered flower onto the ground.

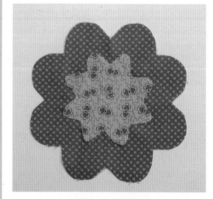

1

2

3

4

5

Achieving Sharp Points

You'll want to make sharp points that lie flat and aren't bulky. Here's how:

1. Stitch toward the point to the exact spot where you wish to turn or change direction. Take an extra stitch at that exact spot to hold it securely.

2. Trim the little protruding point, as well as any excess fabric from the seam allowance, on the side you've just stitched. This ensures that the point will lie flat. To make this delicate work easier, use good-quality, small, sharp-pointed scissors.

3. Turn under the fabric point by catching and rolling the tip of the fabric with the tip of the needle.

4. Tug the thread slightly, directly away from the point. This step pulls any extra fabric out, making the point as sharp as possible.

5. Take a stitch at the tip of the point, and then slip the needle through the thread loop to form a knot. The knot secures the tip and actually makes it appear sharper. Continue stitching down the opposite side of the appliqué patch.

Adding Reverse Appliqué

Even when used sparingly, reverse appliqué adds dramatic dimension to a quilt. I complete the reverse appliquéd area first and then appliqué the patch to the ground.

1. Cut the primary shape where you want the secondary color to show through, allowing for an approximate 3/16″ seam allowance.

2. Cut an oversize piece of the secondary color. I cut the secondary color on the large side, because then I know I'll have plenty to work with and don't need to worry about careful placement.

3. Lay the right side of the secondary piece on the back of the primary patch and baste it just enough to hold it in place. Roll under the raw edge of the primary piece with your needle. Appliqué it down to the secondary piece. Use thread to match the primary piece.

4. When the reverse appliqué is complete, trim the secondary fabric 1/4″ from the stitches.

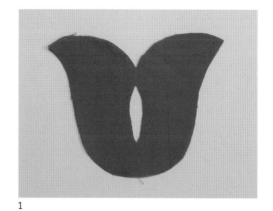

1

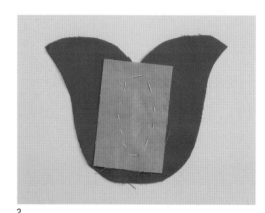

2

3

4

Making Stems

Stems lie flatter and curve more easily when they are cut from the bias of the fabric rather than from the straight of the goods.

A true bias is cut on a 45° angle, but cutting a true bias isn't necessary. Any angle will have give and stretch. I simply lay my ruler at a diagonal that looks about right and use a rotary cutter to cut the required number of strips in the desired width. To make $\frac{5}{8}$″ finished bias, cut bias strips $1\frac{1}{4}$″ wide with a rotary cutter and ruler. Join the strips with diagonal seams, as shown, to make longer strips as needed.

Machine baste the edges under, using my quick and efficient method.

1. Set the machine stitch at the longest length, such as the basting stitch. Fold both long raw edges of the strip inward (wrong sides together) for the first 3″, overlapping them slightly. You don't need to press.

I like to design leaf and flower appliqués to fit snugly against, but not underneath, the stems. This makes the appliqué process easier, because I can complete the stems and then add the additional shapes one at a time instead of basting them all in place. The pieces don't fray, the needle doesn't catch on the basted pieces, and the quilt is far less cumbersome to handle.

2. Stitch 3″, stop, fold the next 3″, and resume sewing. Continue until the entire strip is basted, and then press. Once the stems are appliquéd, you can easily remove the basting stitches.

Machine Appliqué

Although I have never made an entire quilt with machine appliqué, I do use it sparingly when it seems both practical and appropriate. I do not try to do small shapes, sharp curves, or sharp points with the method I use.

This method works well for the straight or slightly curved stems that appear in many of the quilts in this book. Make bias stems as described in Making Stems (page 13). Position and pin the stems to the ground fabric, placing the pins 2″ to 2½″ apart and perpendicular to the stems. Set your machine for a small straight stitch. Using thread to match, secure the stems by stitching very close to one edge, removing pins as you come to them. Repeat to sew the opposite edge of the stems. The previous stitching holds the stems in place, so you won't need to replace the pins before you sew along the other side.

Making Berries

I make berries using the yo-yo method. This method makes it easy to sew the berries to the quilt, because the edges are already finished. I also like that the appliquéd berries look padded.

1. Baste around the edge of the cut circle as shown.

1

2. Place your little finger in the center of the circle and pull the thread around it as shown. Secure it with a knot.

3. Work the gathered fabric into a circle, using the tip of your needle to shape the edges into a smooth curve. (Sometimes I press the berries, and sometimes I don't.)

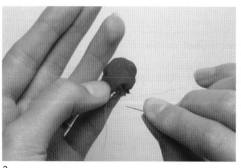

2

3

Gwenny's Goody

I often use a large spool of thread as a template to cut the berries for my quilts. I then fold the fabric in four layers so I can cut four berries at a time.

Projects

Bouquet of Yellow Flowers

Bouquet of Yellow Flowers, 18″ × 20″, designed and made by Gwen Marston, 1997. This quilt looks more complicated than some of the others, but it is not. All the flowers are made from one shape, making it an easy quilt to cut and stitch.

Materials

Yardages are based on fabric that measures 40″ wide after laundering.

- $\frac{7}{8}$ yard muslin for background and binding
- 9″ × 9″ scrap of black swirly print for vase appliqués (A and B)
- Fat quarter (18″ × 21″) dark green solid for stems
- Fat quarter bright yellow print for flower appliqués (C)
- Small scraps of red solid for flower center appliqués (D)
- Fat eighth (9″ × 21″) dark blue print for leaf appliqués (E)
- $\frac{2}{3}$ yard fabric for backing
- 22″ × 24″ piece of batting

Cutting

Cut strips across the fabric width (selvage to selvage) unless otherwise noted. Patterns for appliqué shapes (A–E) appear on page 17.

From the muslin:
Cut 1 piece 18½″ × 20½″.
Cut 3 strips 1¼″ × 40″.

From the black swirly print scrap:
Cut 2 A.
Cut 1 B.

From the dark green solid:
Cut 1¼″-wide strips from the bias of the fabric. You will need 55″ of bias for the stems.

From the bright yellow print:
Cut 11 C.

From the red solid scraps:
Cut 3 D.

From the dark blue print:
Cut 10 E.

Appliquéing and Finishing the Quilt

Refer to Appliqué Basics (pages 6–14), the quilt photo (page 17), and the quilt diagram (below) as needed for guidance with technique and placement.

1. Use your preferred method to place and appliqué 2 A and 1 B to the $18\frac{1}{2}'' \times 20\frac{1}{2}''$ muslin block.

2. Refer to Making Stems (page 13), and use the $1\frac{1}{4}''$-wide dark green solid strips to make a single strip $\frac{5}{8}'' \times 55''$.

3. Using the strip from Step 2, trim, place, and appliqué 5 stems to the block.

4. Place and appliqué 11 C, 3 D, and 10 E to the block.

5. Refer to Finishing Your Quilt (pages 70–73) to layer, baste, and quilt your quilt. Use the $1\frac{1}{4}''$ muslin strips for binding.

Quilt diagram

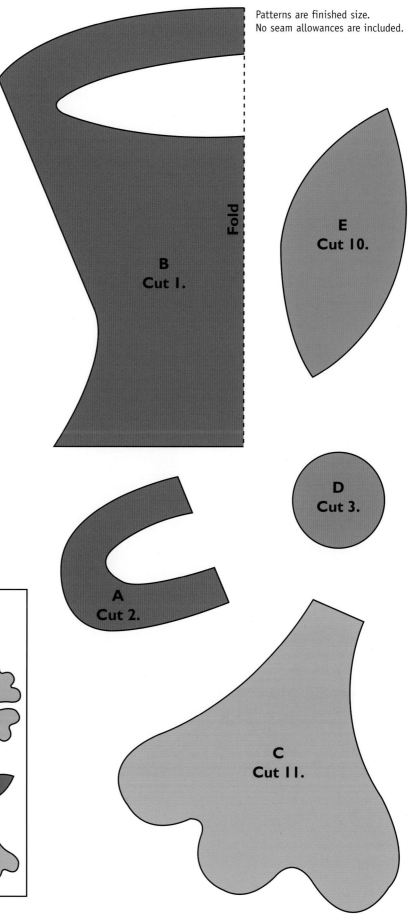

Patterns are finished size.
No seam allowances are included.

B
Cut 1.

Fold

E
Cut 10.

D
Cut 3.

A
Cut 2.

C
Cut 11.

Puppies

Puppies, 16½″ × 20½″, designed and made by Gwen Marston, 1988. What could be more adorable than a group of puppies? This is my version of a popular 1930s commercial pattern of Scottie dogs. It seemed obvious to surround plaid puppies with plaid borders and to quilt the center background with a traditional design called Broken Plaid.

Materials

Yardages are based on fabric that measures 40″ wide after laundering.

- ¼ yard muslin for background
- 6″ × 6″ scraps of 6 assorted plaids for puppy appliqués
- ¼ yard coordinating plaid for border
- ¾ yard fabric for backing
- 21″ × 25″ piece of batting

Cutting

Cut strips across the fabric width (selvage to selvage). The pattern for the puppy appliqué appears on page 19.

From the muslin:
Cut 1 strip 5½″ × 40″; subcut into 6 pieces 6″ × 5½″.

From *each* of the 6 assorted plaid scraps:
Cut 1 puppy appliqué.

From the coordinating plaid:
Cut 2 strips 3″ × 15½″.
Cut 2 strips 3″ × 16½″.

Appliquéing, Assembling, and Finishing the Quilt

Note: Use ¼″-wide seam allowances for all piecing.

Refer to Appliqué Basics (pages 6–14), the quilt photo (page 18), and the block diagram below as needed for guidance with technique and placement.

1. Use your preferred method to place and appliqué 1 puppy appliqué to each 6″ wide × 5½″ long muslin block.

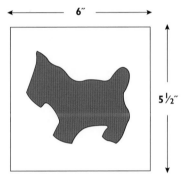

Block diagram

2. Refer to the assembly diagram (at right). Arrange the blocks in 3 horizontal rows of 2 blocks each. Sew the blocks into rows. Press. Sew the rows together. Press.

3. Refer to Borders (page 71). Sew the 3″ × 15½″ plaid borders to the sides of the quilt. Press. Sew the 3″ × 16½″ plaid borders to the top and bottom. Press.

4. Refer to Finishing Your Quilt (pages 70–73) to layer, baste, and quilt your quilt. Finish the edges by folding the backing to the front of the quilt, turning under the raw edge, and machine stitching it in place.

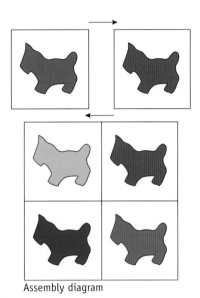

Assembly diagram

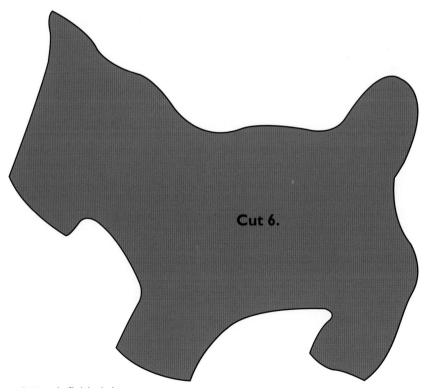

Cut 6.

Pattern is finished size.
No seam allowances are included.

Floral Bouquet in Batiks

Floral Bouquet in Batiks, 18″ × 20″, made by Gwen Marston, 2002. This quilt was a joy to make. Working with beautiful batiks, I used one repeated shape to "grow" my flowers and then arranged them in a simple vase. Appliqué does not need to be complicated or confined to reproduction-style fabrics. It can be both simple and contemporary, as this little quilt attests.

Materials

Yardages are based on fabric that measures 40″ wide after laundering.

- ⁷⁄₈ yard muslin for background and binding
- Fat quarter (18″ × 21″) green batik for stems
- 7″ × 7″ scrap of golden-brown basket-print batik for vase appliqué (A)
- 3″ × 6″ scrap of dark brown geometric-print batik for vase trim appliqués (B, C)
- Assorted black, brown, gold, orange, and peach batik scraps for flower petal appliqués (D, F)
- Small black-and-brown batik print scraps for leaf (E) and flower center (G) appliqués
- ²⁄₃ yard fabric for backing
- 22″ × 24″ piece of batting

Cutting

Cut strips across the fabric width (selvage to selvage) unless otherwise noted. Patterns for appliqué shapes (A–G) appear on page 21.

From the muslin:
Cut 1 piece 18½″ × 20½″.
Cut 3 strips 1¼″ × 40″.

From the green batik:
Cut 1¼″-wide strips from the bias of the fabric. You will need 65″ of bias for the stems.

From the golden-brown basket-print batik scrap:
Cut 1 A.

From the dark brown geometric-print batik scrap:

  Cut 1 *each* of B and C.

From the assorted black, brown, gold, orange, and peach batik scraps:

  Cut 6 D.

  Cut 26 F.

From the black-and-brown batik print scraps:

  Cut 2 E.

  Cut 5 G.

Appliquéing and Finishing the Quilt

Refer to Appliqué Basics (pages 6–14), the quilt photo (page 20), and the quilt diagram (at right) as needed for guidance with technique and placement.

1. Refer to Making Stems (page 13), and use the 1¼″-wide green batik strips to make a single strip ½″ × 65″.

2. Using the strip from Step 1, trim, place, and appliqué 5 stems to the 18½″ × 20½″ muslin block.

3. Use your preferred method to place and appliqué 1 each of A–C, 6 D (in 2 groups of 3 each), and 2 E to the block.

4. Place and appliqué 6 F and 1 G to the end of the top stem and 5 F and 1 G each to the end of the remaining stems.

5. Refer to Finishing Your Quilt (pages 70–73) to layer, baste, and quilt your quilt. Use the 1¼″ muslin strips for binding.

Quilt diagram

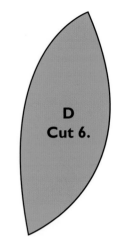

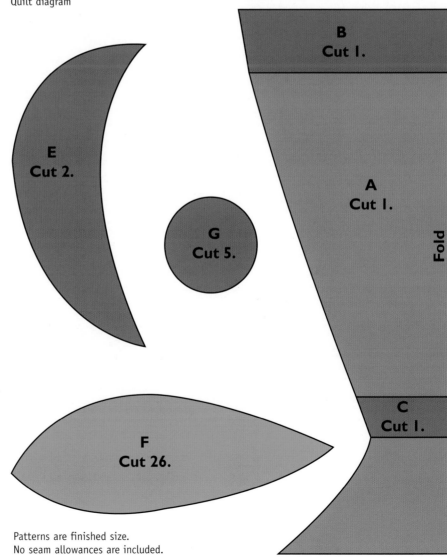

Patterns are finished size.
No seam allowances are included.

Nine-Patch
With Sawtooth Border

Nine-Patch With Sawtooth Border, 18³/₄″ × 22¹/₂″, made by Gwen Marston, 1999. This quilt was made with reproduction fabrics. To create a nineteenth-century scrap-quilt look, I used different fabrics in the alternate plain squares and placed them randomly in the quilt top.

Materials

Yardages are based on fabric that measures 40″ wide after laundering.

- ³/₈ yard *total* assorted light and medium-light prints for Nine-Patch blocks, setting triangles, and sawtooth border
- ²/₃ yard *total* assorted medium-dark and dark prints for Nine-Patch blocks, setting squares, setting triangles, and sawtooth border
- ¼ yard indigo blue print for binding
- ³/₄ yard fabric for backing
- 23″ × 27″ piece of batting

Cutting

Cut strips across the fabric width (selvage to selvage).

From the assorted light and medium-light prints:

Cut 80 squares (total) 1³/₈″ × 1³/₈″ in matching sets of 4.

Cut 2 squares (total) 3¹/₈″ × 3¹/₈″. Cut each square diagonally in one direction to make 2 half-square triangles (4 total).

Cut 20 squares (total) 2³/₄″ × 2³/₄″. Cut each square diagonally in 1 direction to make 2 half-square triangles (40 total).

From the assorted medium-dark and dark prints:

Cut 100 squares (total) 1³/₈″ × 1³/₈″ in matching sets of 5.

Cut 12 squares (total) 3¹/₈″ × 3¹/₈″.

Cut 4 squares (total) 5″ × 5″. Cut each square diagonally in both directions to make 4 quarter-square triangles (16 total). You will have 2 triangles left over.

Cut 20 squares (total) 2¾″ × 2¾″. Cut each square diagonally in 1 direction to make 2 half-square triangles (40 total).

From the indigo blue print:

Cut 3 strips 1¼″ × 40″.

Making the Blocks

Note: Use ¼″-wide seam allowances.

Arrange 4 matching 1⅜″ light or medium-light squares and 5 matching 1⅜″ medium-dark or dark squares in 3 rows as shown. Sew the squares together into rows. Press. Sew the rows together. Press. Make 20.

Make 20.

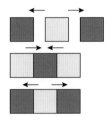

Gwenny's Goody

For an even scrappier look, replace an occasional 1⅜″ light or dark Nine-Patch square with a different print in the same value.

Assembling and Finishing the Quilt

1. Refer to the assembly diagram (at right). Arrange the blocks, 3⅛″ squares, and quarter-square and half-square setting triangles in diagonal rows as shown. Sew the blocks, squares, and quarter-square side triangles into rows. Press. Sew the rows together. Press. Add the half-square corner triangles. Press. Carefully trim the unit to measure 15½″ × 19¼″.

2. Sew light or medium-light triangles and medium-dark or dark triangles in pairs as shown. Press. Make 40.

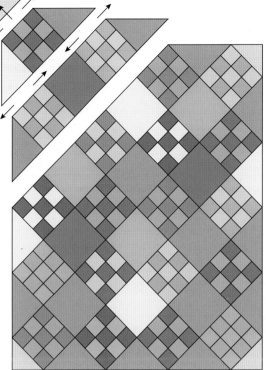

Assembly diagram

Make 40.

3. Sew 10 units from Step 2 together as shown. Press. Make 4.

Make 4.

Gwenny's Goody

To give your quilt even more of a nineteenth-century flavor, rotate some of the half-square sawtooth border units, as shown in the detail at right.

4. Sew a unit from Step 3 to each side of the quilt. Press. Sew the remaining units to the top and bottom. Press.

5. Refer to Finishing Your Quilt (pages 70–73) to layer, baste, and quilt your quilt. Use the 1¼″ indigo blue print strips for binding.

Chicken III

Chicken III, 15½″ × 18½″, designed and made by Gwen Marston, 2003. I liked the idea of using one simple shape for two quite different objects. It's like a cartoon without any words. It makes me happy when my quilts make others smile.

Materials

Yardages are based on fabric that measures 40″ wide after laundering.

- ½ yard light tan small-scale check for background
- 2 bias strips, 1¼″ × 6″, of black star print for chicken legs
- 4″ × 10″ scrap of black multi-colored polka dot for chicken body appliqué (A)
- Small scraps of red solid for comb and tulip appliqués (B)
- 1¼″ × 4½″ bias strip of bright green print for stem
- ½ yard bright yellow and green stripe for side and bottom borders
- 1 strip *each*, 1¾″ × 12¾″, of 2 bright contrasting fabrics for top border
- ⅔ yard fabric for backing

Cutting

Cut strips across the fabric width (selvage to selvage). Patterns for appliqué shapes (A and B) appear on page 25.

From the light tan small-scale check:

Cut 1 piece 12¾″ × 14½″.

From the black multicolored-polka-dot scrap:

Cut 1 A.

From the red solid scraps:

Cut 2 B.

From the bright yellow and green stripe:

Cut 1 strip 2¼″ × 17″.

Cut 1 strip 2″ × 17″.

Cut 1 strip 2½″ × 16″.

From *each* of the 2 bright contrasting fabrics:

Cut 1 strip 1¾″ × 12¾″.

From the backing fabric:

Cut 1 piece 16″ × 19″.

Appliquéing and Finishing the Quilt

Note: Use ¼″-wide seam allowances for all piecing.

Refer to Appliqué Basics (pages 6–14), the quilt photo (page 24), and the quilt diagram (at far right) as needed for guidance with technique and placement.

1. Refer to Making Stems (page 13), and use the 1¼″-wide black star print bias strips to make 2 strips ⅝″ × 6″. Repeat to make a strip ⅝″ × 4½″ using the 1¼″-wide bright green print bias strip.

2. Place and appliqué the black star print strips from Step 1 to the 12¾″ × 14½″ light tan small-scale check block to make chicken legs. Place and appliqué the bright green solid bias strip for the tulip stem.

3. Use your preferred method to place and appliqué 1 A and 2 B to the block.

4. Sew the 2 bright contrasting 1¾″ × 12¾″ strips together along the long edges. Press. Sew to the top of the appliquéd block. Press. Sew the 2¼″ × 17″ bright yellow and green stripe strip to the right side and the 2″ × 17″ bright yellow and green stripe strip to the left side. Press. Sew the 2½″ × 16″ bright yellow and green stripe strip to the bottom. Press.

5. Layer the quilt top and the 16″ × 19″ piece of backing fabric right sides together, carefully aligning the raw edges. Pin. Sew around the outside edges using a ¼″-wide seam. Leave a 4″ opening for turning.

6. Turn the quilt right side out and hand stitch the opening closed.

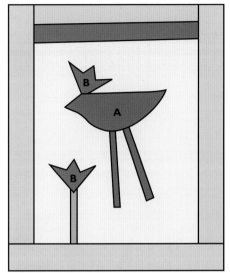

Quilt diagram

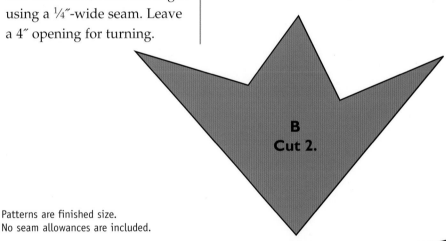

Patterns are finished size.
No seam allowances are included.

B
Cut 2.

A
Cut 1.

Basket With Cherries

Basket With Cherries, 18″ × 20″, designed and made by Gwen Marston, 1991. Much about this quilt is reminiscent of nineteenth-century appliqué in that the stems do not have the same number of leaves, nor are the leaves arranged identically. The same goes for the cherries. The basket isn't symmetrical, and the reverse appliqué on the basket is "casual" … to say the least!

Materials

Yardages are based on fabric that measures 40″ wide after laundering.

- ⅞ yard muslin for background and binding
- Fat quarter (18″ × 21″) red solid for flowerpot (A), bird (B and C), and cherry (D) appliqués
- ⅜ yard green solid for stems and leaf (E) appliqués
- Small scraps of bright yellow solid for reverse appliqué accents
- ⅔ yard fabric for backing
- 22″ × 24″ piece of batting

Cutting

Cut strips across the fabric width (selvage to selvage). Patterns for appliqué shapes (A–E) appear on page 27.

From the muslin:
Cut 1 piece 18½″ × 20½″.
Cut 3 strips 1¼″ × 40″.

From the red solid:
Cut 1 A.
Cut 1 B.
Cut 1 C and 1 C reverse.
Cut 24 D.

From the green solid:
Cut 1″-wide strips from the bias of the fabric. You will need 55″ of bias for the stems.
Cut 26 E.

Appliquéing and Finishing the Quilt

Refer to Appliqué Basics (pages 6–14), the quilt photo (page 26), and the quilt diagram (at right) as needed for guidance with technique and placement.

1. Refer to Adding Reverse Appliqué (page 12), and appliqué the bright yellow solid scraps to piece A.

2. Refer to Making Stems (page 13), and use the 1″-wide green solid strips to make a single strip ¼″ × 55″.

3. Using the strip from Step 2, trim, place, and appliqué 5 stems to the 18½″ × 20½″ muslin block.

4. Use your preferred method to place and appliqué 1 each of A, B, C, and C reverse; 24 D; and 26 E to the block.

5. Refer to Finishing Your Quilt (pages 70–73) to layer, baste, and quilt your quilt. Use the 1¼″ muslin strips for binding.

Quilt diagram

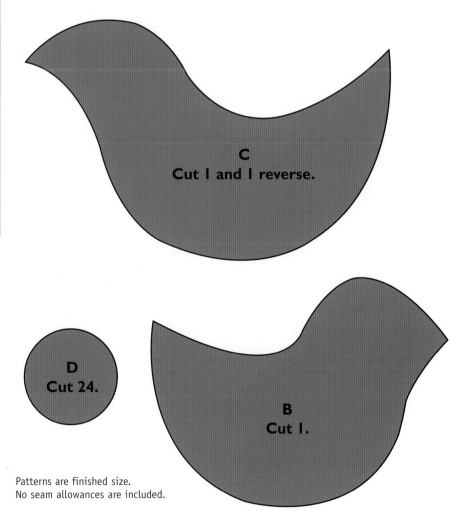

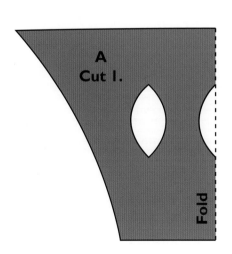

Patterns are finished size.
No seam allowances are included.

Chicken

Chicken, 18″ × 20″, designed and made by Gwen Marston, 1983. I've noticed that quite a number of antique folk-art quilts included words added without preplanning and—as a result—often required "creative adjustment." I've used this idea more than once myself because I like the playful effect.

Materials

Yardages are based on fabric that measures 40″ wide after laundering.

- ⅔ yard light tan small-scale check for background
- ⅜ yard red solid for comb (A) and letter appliqués and binding
- Fat quarter (18″ × 21″) dark brown chicken print for chicken body appliqué (B)
- Small scraps of bright yellow solid for beak (C) and eye (D) appliqués
- ⅔ yard fabric for backing
- 22″ × 24″ piece of batting

Cutting

Cut strips across the fabric width (selvage to selvage). Patterns for appliqué shapes (A–D and letters) appear on pages 29–32.

From the light tan small-scale check:

Cut 1 piece 18½″ × 20½″.

From the red solid:

Cut 1 A.

Cut 1 each of the letters *H, I, K, E,* and *N.*

Cut 2 of the letter *C.*

Cut 3 strips 1¼″ × 40″.

From the dark brown chicken print:

Cut 1 B (B1, B2, and B3).

From the bright yellow scraps:

Cut 1 *each* of C and D.*

If you wish to add the eye with reverse appliqué, as I did, you will not need to cut piece D. Refer to Adding Reverse Appliqué on page 12.

Appliquéing and Finishing the Quilt

Refer to Appliqué Basics (pages 6–14), the quilt photo (page 28), and the quilt diagram (below) as needed for guidance with technique and placement.

1. Use your preferred method to place and appliqué 1 each of A, B, C, and D to the 18½″ × 20½″ light tan small-scale check block. Place and appliqué the letters for the word *CHICKEN*, as shown.

2. Refer to Finishing Your Quilt (pages 70–73) to layer, baste, and quilt your quilt. Use the 1¼″ red solid strips for binding.

Quilt diagram

Patterns are finished size. No seam allowances are included.

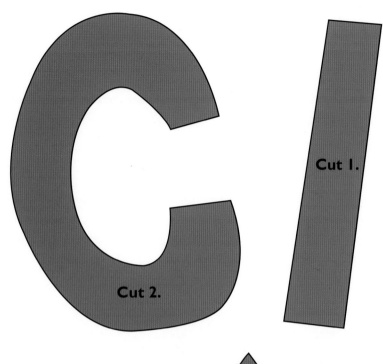

Cut 1.

Cut 2.

A
Cut 1.

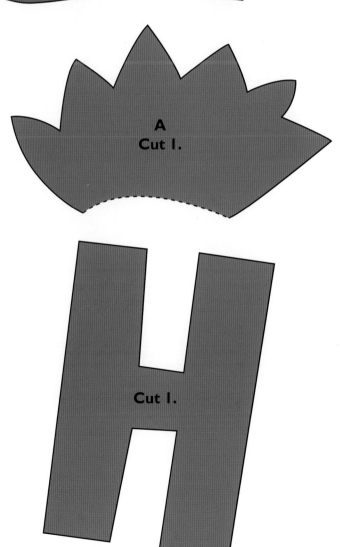

Cut 1.

C
Cut 1.

D
Cut 1.

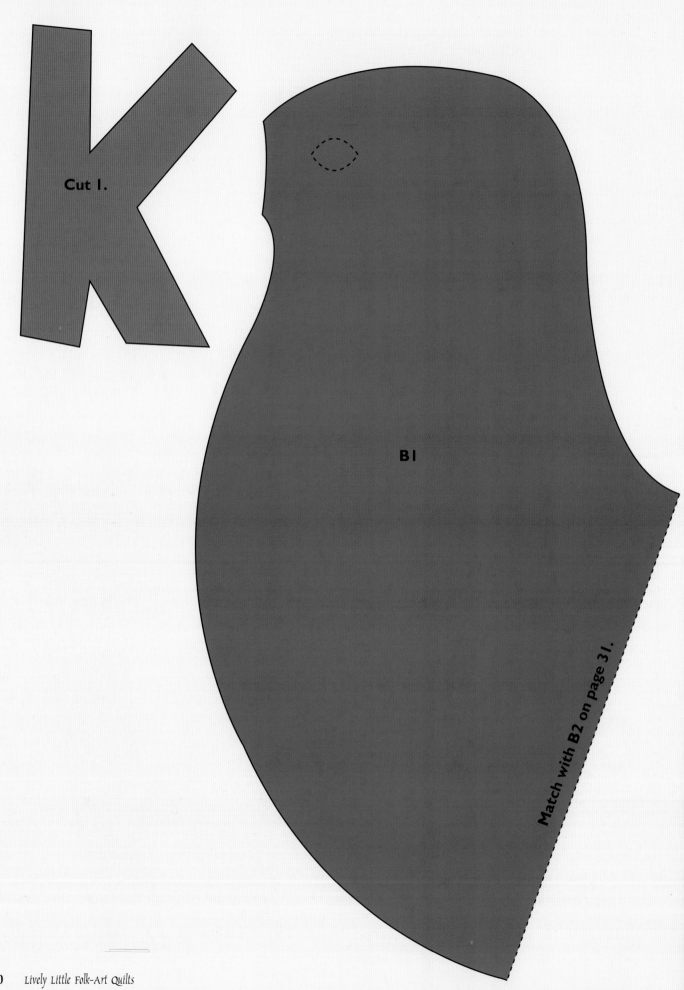

Cut 1.

B1

Match with B2 on page 31.

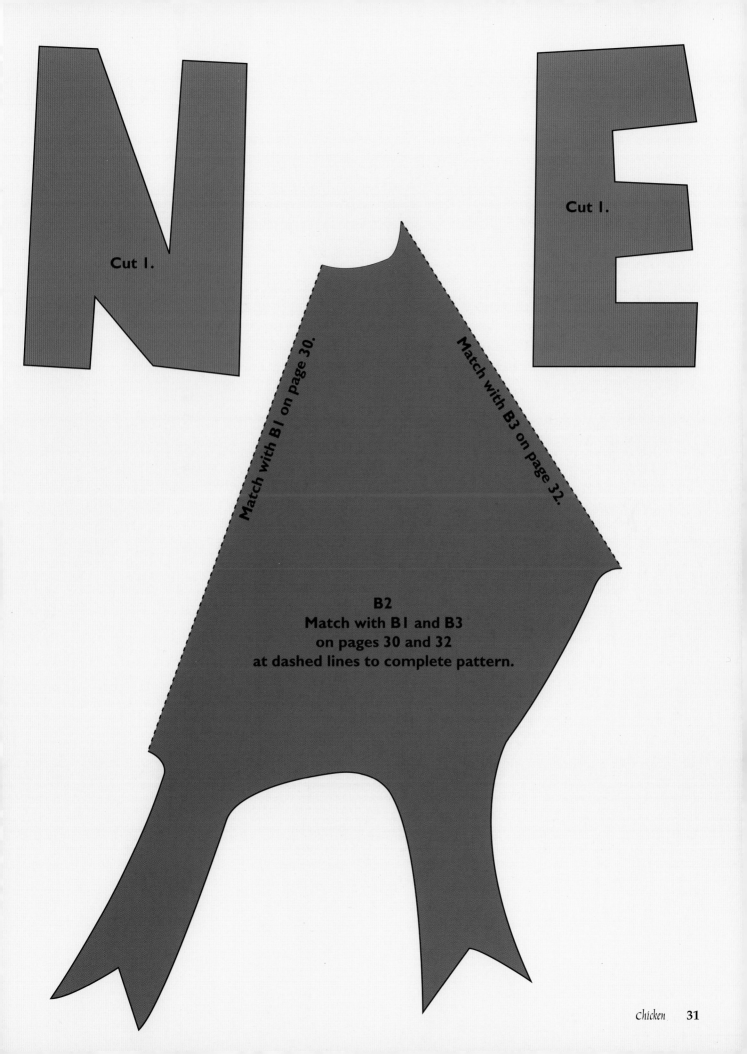

Cut 1.

Cut 1.

Match with B1 on page 30.

Match with B3 on page 32.

B2
Match with B1 and B3
on pages 30 and 32
at dashed lines to complete pattern.

B3

Match with B2 on page 31.

Flowers in Blue Vase

Flowers in Blue Vase, 18″ × 20″, designed and made by Gwen Marston, 1997. In keeping with nineteenth-century appliqué characteristics, I balanced the overall composition but varied the placement of the individual patches. The sharp little points may seem intimidating, but fear not: points are easier to appliqué than curves!

Materials

Yardages are based on fabric that measures 40″ wide after laundering.

- ⅔ yard pink-on-pink small-scale print for background
- Fat quarter (18″ × 21″) dark reddish brown subtle print or solid for stems and leaf appliqués (B)
- 7″ × 9″ scrap of bright blue print for vase appliqué (A)
- ¼ yard *each* of 2 bright red prints for flower appliqués (C–G)
- ¼ yard bright yellow print for flower appliqués (H–J) and reverse appliqué accents
- Scraps of purple print for flower appliqués (K)
- ¼ yard medium blue print for binding
- ⅔ yard fabric for backing
- 22″ × 24″ piece of batting

Cutting

Cut strips across the fabric width (selvage to selvage). Patterns for appliqué shapes (A–K) appear on pages 34–35.

From the pink-on-pink small-scale print:

Cut 1 piece 18½″ × 20½″.

From the dark reddish brown subtle print or solid:

Cut 1¼″-wide strips from the bias of the fabric. You will need 40″ of bias for the stems.

Cut 5 B.

From the bright blue print scrap:
 Cut 1 A.

From bright red print #1:
 Cut 2 C and 2 C reverse.

From bright red print #2:
 Cut 2 D.
 Cut 1 *each* of E–G.

From the bright yellow print:
 Cut 1 *each* of H–J.

From the purple print scraps:
 Cut 2 K.

From the medium blue print:
 Cut 3 strips 1¼″ × 40″.

Appliquéing and Finishing the Quilt

Refer to Appliqué Basics (pages 6–14), the quilt photo (page 33), and the quilt diagram (at far right) as needed for guidance with technique and placement.

1. Refer to Making Stems (page 13), and use the 1¼″-wide dark reddish brown subtle print strips to make a single strip ⅝″ × 40″.

2. Using the strip from Step 1, trim, place, and appliqué 5 stems to the 18½″ × 20½″ pink-on-pink small-scale print block.

3. Use your preferred method to place and appliqué 1 A, 5 B, 4 C, 2 D, and 1 each of E–J to the block.

4. Refer to Adding Reverse Appliqué (page 12), and appliqué a remaining bright yellow print scrap to each piece K. Appliqué to the block.

5. Refer to Finishing Your Quilt (pages 70–73) to layer, baste, and quilt your quilt. Use the 1¼″ medium blue print strips for binding.

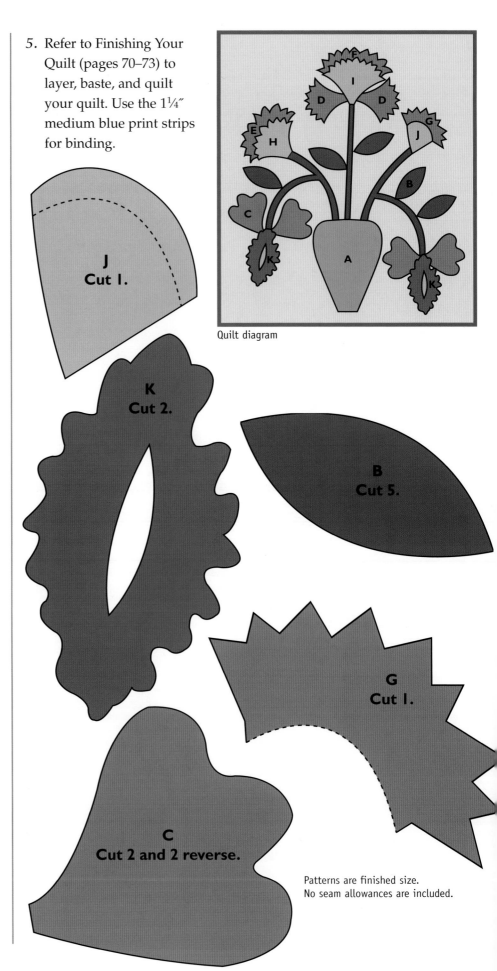

Quilt diagram

J
Cut 1.

K
Cut 2.

B
Cut 5.

G
Cut 1.

C
Cut 2 and 2 reverse.

Patterns are finished size.
No seam allowances are included.

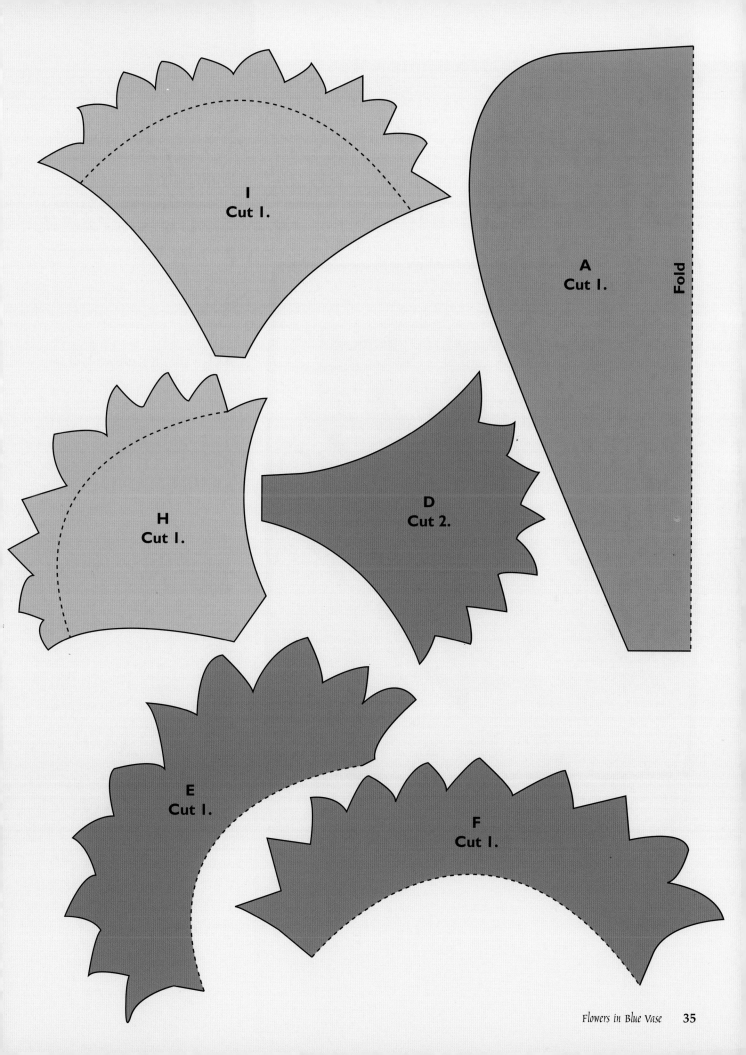

I
Cut 1.

A
Cut 1.

Fold

H
Cut 1.

D
Cut 2.

E
Cut 1.

F
Cut 1.

Flower Pot

Flower Pot, 17½″ × 20″, made by Gwen Marston, 1998. The baskets in this little scrap quilt were made with hand-dyed fabrics and commercial prints on a tan small-scale background.

Materials

Yardages are based on fabric that measures 40″ wide after laundering.

- ⅔ yard light tan small-scale check for background
- ⅜ yard *total* assorted medium and dark prints and solids for blocks
- ¼ yard dark green solid for binding
- ⅔ yard fabric for backing
- 22″ × 24″ piece of batting

Cutting

Cut strips across the fabric width (selvage to selvage).

From the light tan small-scale check:

Cut 9 squares 1⅞″ × 1⅞″. Cut each square diagonally in 1 direction to make 2 half-square triangles (A) (18 total).

Cut 5 squares 3¼″ × 3¼″. Cut each square diagonally in both directions to make 4 quarter-square triangles (B) (20 total). You will have 2 triangles left over.

Cut 5 squares 2⅞″ × 2⅞″. Cut each square diagonally in 1 direction to make 2 half-square triangles (C) (10 total). You will have 1 triangle left over.

Cut 9 squares 1½″ × 1½″ (D).

Cut 2 strips 1½″ × 40″; subcut into 18 strips 1½″ × 3½″ (E).

Cut 2 strips 1½″ × 15½″.

Cut 2 strips 2½″ × 17½″.

From the assorted medium and dark prints and solids:

Cut 27 squares (total) $1\frac{7}{8}'' \times 1\frac{7}{8}''$. Cut each square diagonally in 1 direction to make 2 half-square triangles (A) (54 total).

Cut 23 squares (total) $2\frac{7}{8}'' \times 2\frac{7}{8}''$. Cut each square diagonally in 1 direction to make 2 half-square triangles (C) (46 total). You will have 1 triangle left over.

From the dark green solid:

Cut 3 strips $1\frac{1}{4}'' \times 40''$.

Making the Blocks

Note: Use $\frac{1}{4}''$-wide seam allowances.

1. Sew light tan small-scale check A triangles and print or solid A triangles in pairs as shown. Press. Make 18.

Make 18.

2. Sew a print or solid A triangle to a light tan small-scale check B triangle as shown. Press. Make 9 of each.

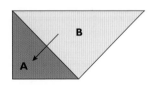

Make 9 each.

3. Sew a unit from Step 1 to a unit from Step 2 as shown. Press. Make 9 of each.

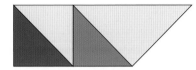

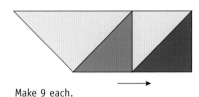

Make 9 each.

4. Sew a unit from Step 3 to a print or solid C triangle as shown. Press. Make 9.

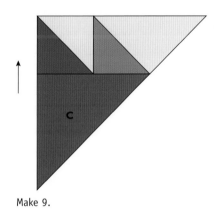

Make 9.

5. Sew a $1\frac{1}{2}''$ light tan small-scale check D square to a remaining unit from Step 3 as shown. Press. Sew to a unit from Step 4. Press. Make 9.

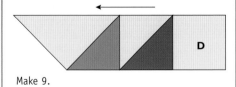

Make 9.

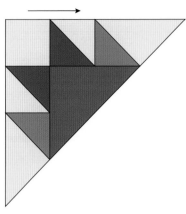

Make 9.

6. Sew 2 print or solid C triangles together as shown. Press. Sew a print or solid C triangle to adjacent sides of the unit. Press. Make 9.

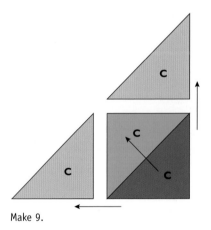

Make 9.

7. Sew a remaining print or solid A triangle to each 1½″ × 3½″ light tan small-scale check E strip as shown. Press. Make 9 of each. Sew 1 of each pieced strip to opposite sides of each unit from Step 6. Press. Make 9.

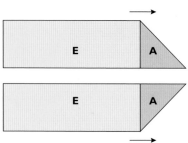

Make 9 each.

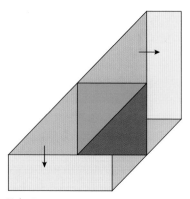

Make 9.

8. Sew a light tan small-scale check C triangle to each unit from Step 7 as shown. Press. Make 9.

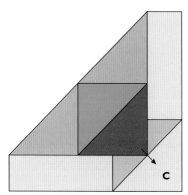

Make 9.

9. Sew a unit from Step 5 to a unit from Step 8 as shown. Press. Make 9.

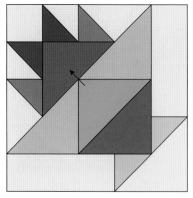

Make 9.

Assembling and Finishing the Quilt

1. Refer to the assembly diagram below. Arrange the blocks in 3 horizontal rows of 3 blocks each. Sew the blocks into rows. Press. Sew the rows together. Press.

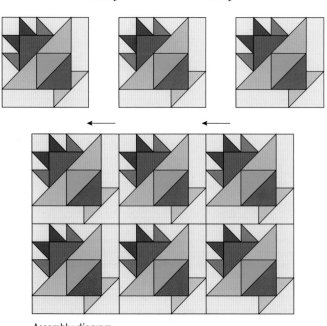

Assembly diagram

2. Refer to Borders (page 71). Sew the 1½″ × 15½″ light tan small-scale check borders to the sides of the quilt. Press. Sew the 2½″ × 17½″ light tan small-scale check borders to the top and bottom. Press.

3. Refer to Finishing Your Quilt (pages 70–73) to layer, baste, and quilt your quilt. Use the 1¼″ dark green solid fabric strips for binding.

Thistles

Thistles, 18″ × 20″, designed and made by Gwen Marston, 2003. If you have seen healthy thistles thriving in the wild, you will always appreciate their impressive beauty. Although they are not usually seen in bouquets, I brought these beauties inside and put them in this quilt for all to enjoy.

Materials

Yardages are based on fabric that measures 40″ wide after laundering.

- ¾ yard muslin for background and binding
- ⅜ yard medium-dark green print for stems and leaf (B) and thistle cup (D) appliqués
- 7″ × 7″ scrap of pink-and-white print for vase appliqué (A)
- ¼ yard pink small-scale print for thistle appliqués (C)
- ⅔ yard fabric for backing
- 22″ × 24″ piece of batting

Cutting

Cut strips across the fabric width (selvage to selvage) unless otherwise noted. Patterns for appliqué shapes (A–D) appear on page 41.

From the muslin:
    Cut 1 piece 18½″ × 20½″.
    Cut 3 strips 1¼″ × 40″.

From the medium-dark green print:
    Cut 1¼″-wide strips from the bias of the fabric. You will need 40″ of bias for the stems.
    Cut 1 B and 1 B reverse.
    Cut 6 D.

From the pink-and-white print scrap:
    Cut 1 A.

From the pink small-scale print:
    Cut 6 C.

Appliquéing and Finishing the Quilt

Refer to Appliqué Basics (pages 6–14), the quilt photo (page 39), and the quilt diagram (at right) as needed for guidance with technique and placement.

1. Refer to Making Stems (page 13), and use the 1¼″-wide medium-dark green print strips to make a single strip ⅝″ × 40″.

2. Using the strip from Step 1, trim, place, and appliqué 6 stems to the 18½″ × 20½″ muslin block.

3. Use your preferred method to place and appliqué 1 each of B and B reverse, 6 C, and 6 D to the block.

4. Refer to Finishing Your Quilt (pages 70–73) to layer, baste, and quilt your quilt. Use the 1¼″ muslin strips for binding.

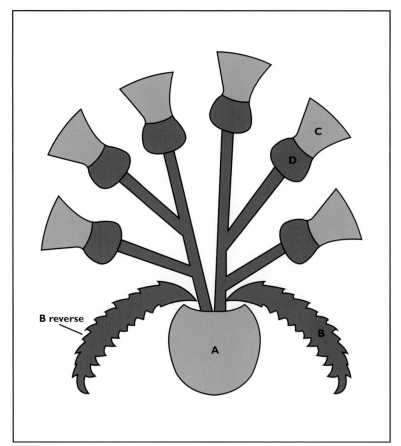

Quilt diagram

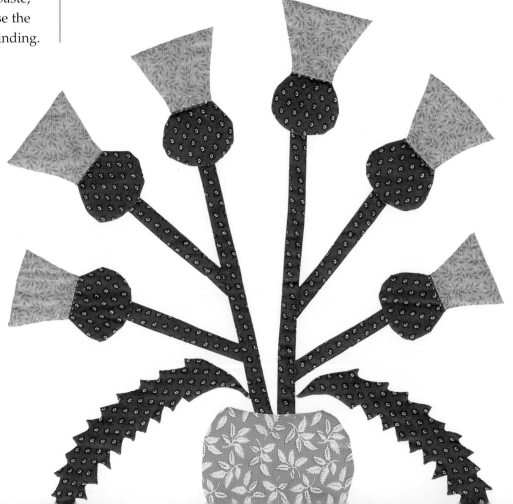

Patterns are finished size.
No seam allowances are included.

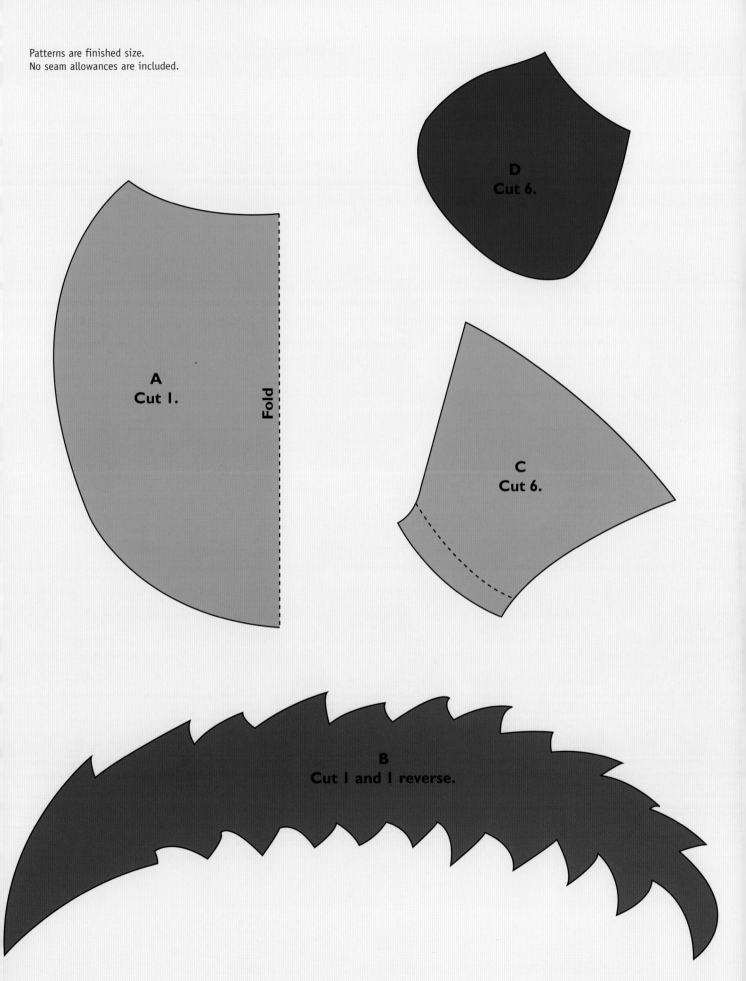

D
Cut 6.

A
Cut 1.

Fold

C
Cut 6.

B
Cut 1 and 1 reverse.

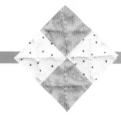

Four-Patch With Streak o' Lightning

Four-Patch With Streak o' Lightning, 17½″ × 20½″, designed and made by Gwen Marston, 1995. These four-patches rest on point in an old-fashioned setting called Zig Zag or Streak o' Lightning. As you can see, the set is very dramatic when the side triangles are cut from a high-contrast color like acid green against the bubble-gum pink borders.

Materials

Yardages are based on fabric that measures 40″ wide after laundering.

- ¼ yard *total* assorted white prints for blocks
- ¼ yard *total* assorted pink prints for blocks
- ¼ yard yellow print for blocks and binding
- ⅓ yard acid green print for setting triangles
- ¼ yard pink print for border*
- ¾ yard fabric for backing
- 22″ × 25″ piece of batting

May be one of the assorted pink prints.

Cutting

Cut strips across the fabric width (selvage to selvage).

From the assorted white prints:

Cut *a total of* 36 squares 1¾″ × 1¾″ in matching pairs (A).

Cut *a total of* 2 squares 2⅝″ × 2⅝″. Cut each square diagonally in both directions to make 4 quarter-square triangles (8 total) (B).

From the assorted pink prints:

Cut *a total of* 34 squares 1¾″ × 1¾″ in matching pairs (A).

From the yellow print:

Cut 6 squares 1¾″ × 1¾″ (A).
Cut 3 strips 1¼″ × 40″.

From the acid green print:

Cut 2 strips 4¾″ × 40″; subcut into 9 squares 4¾″ × 4¾″. Cut each square diagonally in both directions to make 4 quarter-square triangles (36 total) (C).

Cut 4 squares 2¾″ × 2¾″. Cut each square diagonally in 1 direction to make 2 half-square triangles (8 total) (D).

From the pink print:
Cut 2 strips 2″ × 18″.
Cut 2 strips 2″ × 17½″.

Making the Blocks and Rows

Note: Use ¼″-wide seam allowances.

1. Arrange 2 matching white print A squares and 2 matching pink print A squares as shown. Sew the squares together into rows. Press. Sew the rows together. Press. Make 15.

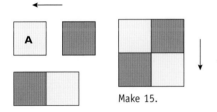

Make 15.

2. Repeat Step 1 using the remaining white print A squares and the yellow print A squares. Make 3.

Make 3.

3. Sew a white print B triangle to 2 adjacent sides of each remaining pink print A square as shown. Press. Make 4.

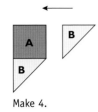

Make 4.

4. Sew 2 acid green print C triangles to opposite sides of a block from Step 1, taking care to orient the block and the triangles as shown. Press. Make 11.

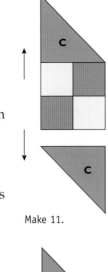

Make 11.

5. Repeat Step 4 using the blocks from Step 2. Make 3.

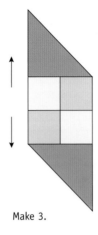

Make 3.

6. Sew 2 acid green print D triangles and 1 acid green print C triangle to each remaining block from Step 1. Press. Make 4.

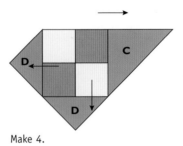

Make 4.

7. Sew a remaining acid green print C triangle to each unit from Step 3 as shown. Press. Make 4.

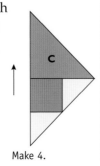

Make 4.

8. Arrange and sew the units from Steps 4–7 together to make 4 rows, taking care to place the units as shown in the assembly diagram (below). Press.

Assembling and Finishing the Quilt

1. Refer to the assembly diagram below. Arrange and sew the 4 rows together. Press. Trim to 14½″ × 18″.

2. Refer to Borders (page 71). Sew the 2″ × 18″ pink print borders to the sides of the quilt. Press. Sew the 2″ × 17½″ pink print borders to the top and bottom. Press.

3. Refer to Finishing Your Quilt (pages 70–73) to layer, baste, and quilt your quilt. Use the 1¼″ yellow print strips for binding.

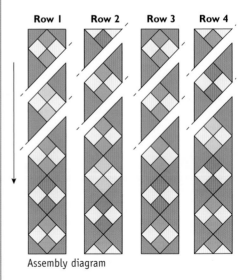

Assembly diagram

Texas Longhorn

Texas Longhorn, 21″ × 18″, designed and made by Gwen Marston, 1994. I'm an animal lover, and animals frequently show up in my quilts. I prefer to have my longhorn safely confined, so I sewed him into this quilt. I remember hearing a story about being chased by a bull. The tale ended with the sage acknowledgment that when a bull is chasing you, a tie at the fence is the same as a loss.

Materials

Yardages are based on fabric that measures 40″ wide after laundering.

- ⅔ yard light tan small-scale check for background
- 6″ × 6″ scrap of black solid for bull's horns (A), eye (C), and tail (D) appliqués
- Fat quarter (18″ × 21″) bright red solid for bull's body (B) and tulip (F) appliqués
- Small scrap of white solid for bull's eye reverse appliqué
- Small scraps of bright green solid for stem and tulip leaf (E) appliqués
- 6″ × 5″ scrap of bright yellow solid for bird appliqué (G)
- 7″ × 5″ scrap of bright blue solid for bird appliqué (H)
- ¼ yard dark brown small-scale check for binding
- ⅔ yard fabric for backing
- 25″ × 22″ piece of batting
- Black embroidery floss

Cutting

Cut strips across the fabric width (selvage to selvage). Patterns for appliqué shapes (A–H) appear on pages 45–47.

From the light tan small-scale check:

Cut 1 piece 21½″ × 18½″.

From the black solid scrap:

Cut 2 A.

Cut 1 *each* of C and D.

From the bright red solid:

Cut 1 B (B1, B2, and B3).

Cut 1 F.

From the bright green solid scraps:*

Cut 1 bias strip 1¼″ × 3½″.
Cut 2 E.

From the bright yellow solid scrap:

Cut 1 G.

From the bright blue solid scrap:

Cut 1 H.

From the dark brown small-scale check:

Cut 3 strips 1¼″ × 40″.

You can use 2 different greens: one for the stem and one for the leaves.

Appliquéing and Finishing the Quilt

Refer to Appliqué Basics (pages 6–14), the quilt photo (page 44), and the quilt diagram (at far right) as needed for guidance with technique and placement.

1. Refer to Adding Reverse Appliqué (page 12), and appliqué a white solid scrap to piece B for the eye.

2. Use your preferred method to place and appliqué 2 A, 1 B with reverse appliqué, and 1 each of C and D to the 21½″ × 18½″ light tan small-scale check block.

3. Refer to Making Stems (page 13), and use the 1¼″-wide bright green solid strip to make a single strip ½″ × 3½″.

4. Place and appliqué the strip from Step 3, 2 E, and 1 F to the block.

5. Place and appliqué 1 each of G and H to the block.

6. Use 2 strands of black embroidery floss and a stem stitch to embroider the long bull tail.

Stem stitch

7. Refer to Finishing Your Quilt (pages 70–73) to layer, baste, and quilt your quilt. Use the 1¼″ dark brown small-scale check strips for binding.

Quilt diagram

Match with B2 on page 47.

B1

C
Cut 1.

E
Cut 2.

D
Cut 1.

Patterns are finished size.
No seam allowances are included.

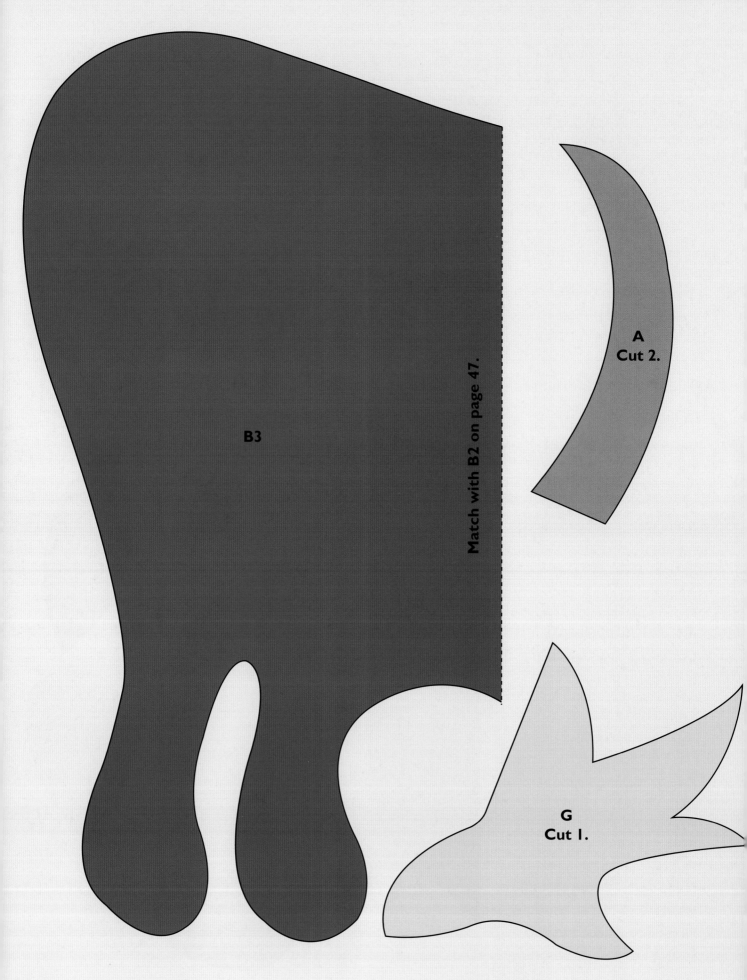

B3

Match with B2 on page 47.

A
Cut 2.

G
Cut 1.

F
Cut 1.

Match with B1 on page 45.

Match with B3 on page 46.

B2
Match with B1 and B3 on pages 45 and 46
at dashed lines to complete pattern.

H
Cut 1.

Lady of the Lake Variation

Lady of the Lake Variation, 15″ × 18″, designed and made by Gwen Marston, 1995. Here is a formula that always works: a classic pattern worked in a classic color scheme—in this case, blue and white.

Materials

Yardages are based on fabric that measures 40″ wide after laundering.

- ½ yard muslin for blocks and binding
- ½ yard indigo blue print for blocks
- ⅔ yard fabric for backing
- 19″ × 22″ piece of batting

Cutting

Cut strips across the fabric width (selvage to selvage).

From the muslin:

Cut 4 strips 1⅞″ × 40″; subcut into 75 squares 1⅞″ × 1⅞″. Cut each square diagonally in 1 direction to make 2 half-square triangles (A) (150 total).

Cut 2 strips 2⅞″ × 40″; subcut into 15 squares 2⅞″ × 2⅞″. Cut each square diagonally in 1 direction to make 2 half-square triangles (B) (30 total).

Cut 2 strips 1¼″ × 40″.

From the indigo blue print:

Cut 4 strips 1⅞″ × 40″; subcut into 75 squares 1⅞″ × 1⅞″. Cut each square diagonally in 1 direction to make 2 half-square triangles (A) (150 total).

Cut 2 strips 2⅞″ × 40″; subcut into 15 squares 2⅞″ × 2⅞″. Cut each square diagonally in 1 direction to make 2 half-square triangles (B) (30 total).

Making the Blocks

Note: Use ¼″-wide seam allowances.

1. Sew muslin A triangles and indigo blue print A triangles in pairs as shown. Press. Make 90.

Make 90.

2. Sew an indigo blue print A triangle to a unit from Step 1 as shown. Press. Make 30.

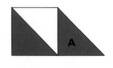

Make 30.

3. Sew a unit from Step 1 between an indigo blue print A triangle and a muslin A triangle as shown. Press. Make 30.

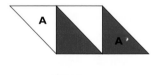

Make 30.

4. Sew a unit from Step 1 to a muslin A triangle as shown. Press. Make 30.

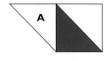

Make 30.

5. Sew a unit from Step 3 between a unit from Step 2 and a unit from Step 4 as shown. Press. Make 30.

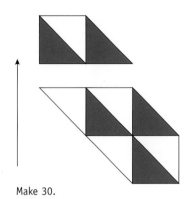

Make 30.

6. Sew a muslin B triangle and an indigo blue print B triangle to each unit from Step 5. Press. Make 30.

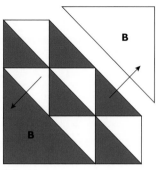

Make 30.

Assembling and Finishing the Quilt

1. Refer to the assembly diagram below. Arrange the blocks in 6 horizontal rows of 5 blocks each. Sew the blocks into rows. Press. Sew the rows together. Press.

2. Refer to Finishing Your Quilt (pages 70–73) to layer, baste, and quilt your quilt. Use the 1¼″ muslin strips for binding.

Assembly diagram

Gwenny's Basket

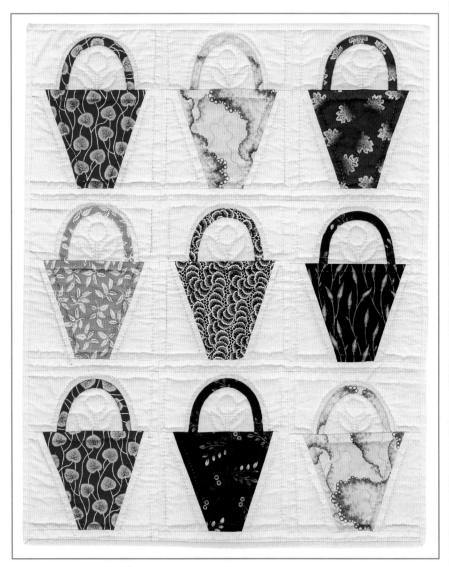

Gwenny's Basket, 18½" × 23", designed and made by Gwen Marston, 1999. I have always preferred simple, direct design. Here is my own pattern, and it is about as simple and direct as you can get. This is a good pattern for showcasing your favorite prints, because the body of the basket is made from a single fabric shape.

Materials

Yardages are based on fabric that measures 40" wide after laundering.

- ¾ yard muslin for background and binding
- Fat eighths (9" × 21") or large scraps (at least 8" × 10") of 9 assorted prints for basket and handle appliqués*
- ¾ yard fabric for backing
- 23" × 27" piece of batting

*If you like, you can duplicate some of the prints, as I did.

Cutting

Cut strips across the fabric width (selvage to selvage). Patterns for pieces A and B appear on page 51.

From the muslin:

Cut 2 strips 3" × 40"; subcut into 9 pieces 3" × 6½".

Cut 2 strips 1" × 40"; subcut into 9 strips 1" × 6½".

Cut 9 *each* B and B reverse.

Cut 3 strips 1¼" × 40".

From each of the 9 assorted print fat eighths or scraps:

Cut 1 A.

Cut 1 bias strip 1¼" × 6".

Making and Appliquéing the Blocks

Note: Use ¼"-wide seam allowances for piecing.

Refer to Appliqué Basics (pages 6–14), the quilt photo (at left), and the assembly diagram (page 51) as needed for guidance with technique and placement.

1. Sew piece A between 1 piece B and piece B reverse as shown. Press. Make 9.

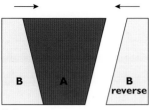

Make 9.

2. Refer to Making Stems (page 13), and use each 1¼″-wide assorted print bias strip to make a strip ½″ × 6″.

3. Use your preferred method to appliqué a strip from Step 2 to each 3″ × 6½″ muslin piece.

4. Sew a unit from Step 1 between the matching-fabric unit from Step 3 and a 1″ × 6½″ muslin strip as shown. Press. Make 9.

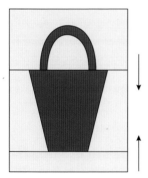

Make 9.

Assembling and Finishing the Quilt

1. Refer to the assembly diagram (at right). Arrange the blocks in 3 horizontal rows of 3 blocks each. Sew the blocks into rows. Press. Sew the rows together. Press.

2. Refer to Finishing Your Quilt (pages 70–73) to layer, baste, and quilt your quilt. Use the 1¼″ muslin strips for binding.

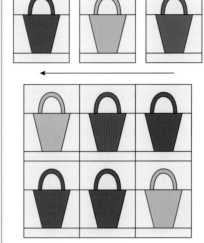

Assembly diagram

Patterns include ¼″-wide seam allowance.

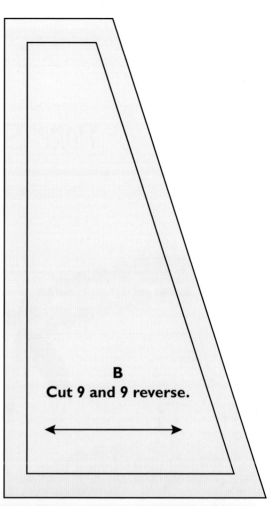

B
Cut 9 and 9 reverse.

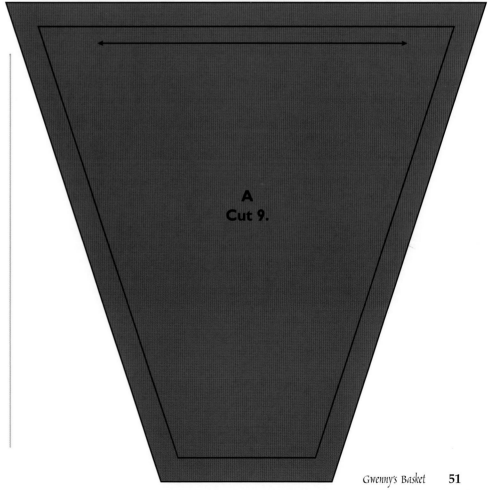

A
Cut 9.

Poke Stalk

Poke Stalk, 18″ × 20″, designed and made by Gwen Marston, 1994. This quilt was inspired by a very appealing quilt made by Elizabeth Currier, who traveled over the Oregon Trail in 1845. I was so drawn to Elizabeth's quilt that I started making mine about fifteen minutes after I first saw a photo of the original. Elizabeth's quilt is shown in *Treasures in the Trunk: Quilts of the Oregon Trail,* by Mary Bywater Cross, and in Jeana Kimball's *Red and Green: An Appliqué Tradition* (see Bibliography on page 79).

Materials

Yardages are based on fabric that measures 40″ wide after laundering.

- ⅞ yard muslin for background and binding
- Fat quarter (18″ × 21″) bright cheddar-gold subtle print for stalks
- ⅛ yard dark green subtle print for leaf appliqués (A)
- ⅛ yard *total* of assorted red solid scraps for berry appliqués (B)
- ⅔ yard fabric for backing
- 22″ × 24″ piece of batting

Cutting

Cut strips across the fabric width (selvage to selvage). Patterns for appliqué shapes (A and B) appear on page 53.

From the muslin:
Cut 1 piece 18½″ × 20½″.
Cut 3 strips 1¼″ × 40″.

From the bright cheddar-gold subtle print:
Cut 1¼″-wide strips from the bias of the fabric. You will need 42″ of bias for the stalks.

From the dark green subtle print:
Cut 7 A.

From the red solid scraps:
Cut *a total of* 55 B.

Appliquéing and Finishing the Quilt

Refer to Appliqué Basics (pages 6–14), the quilt photo (page 52), and the quilt diagram (at right) as needed for guidance with technique and placement.

1. Refer to Making Stems (page 13), and use the 1¼″-wide bright cheddar-gold subtle print strips to make a strip ½″ × 42″.

2. Using the strip from Step 1, trim, place, and appliqué 3 stalks to the 18½″ × 20½″ muslin block.

3. Use your preferred method to place and appliqué 7 A to the block.

4. Place and appliqué 55 B to the 3 stalks, randomly mixing the various red solids.

5. Refer to Finishing Your Quilt (pages 70–73) to layer, baste, and quilt your quilt. Use the 1¼″ muslin strips for binding.

Quilt diagram

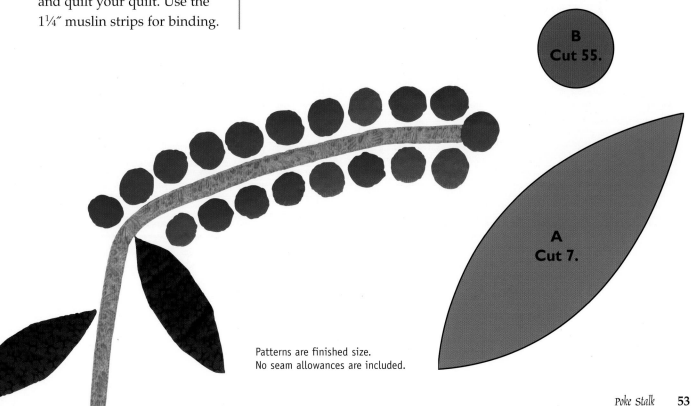

B
Cut 55.

A
Cut 7.

Patterns are finished size.
No seam allowances are included.

Kitty

Kitty, 17″ × 20″, designed and made by Gwen Marston, 1993. Anyone who loves cats would love this quilt. I've embellished it with fuzzy yarn for whiskers and yarn ties to suggest a snuggly, furry friend. As someone told me recently, "Dogs have masters, and cats have staff."

Materials

Yardages are based on fabric that measures 40″ wide after laundering.

- ⅔ yard dark blue multi-colored-speckle print for background
- ½ yard medium pink print for cat appliqué (A) and binding
- Fat quarter (18″ × 21″) bright gold print for moon (B) and star (C) appliqués
- ⅔ yard fabric for backing
- 21″ × 24″ piece of batting
- White yarn
- Pink yarn or embroidery floss

Cutting

Cut strips across the fabric width (selvage to selvage). Patterns for appliqué shapes (A–C) appear on pages 55–57.

From the dark blue multi-colored-speckle print:
Cut 1 piece 17½″ × 20½″.

From the medium pink print:
Cut 1 A (A1 and A2).
Cut 3 strips 1¼″ × 40″.

From the bright gold print:
Cut 1 *each* of B and C.

Appliquéing and Finishing the Quilt

Refer to Appliqué Basics (pages 6–14), the quilt photo (page 54), and the quilt diagram (at right) as needed for guidance with technique and placement.

1. Use your preferred method to place and appliqué 1 each of A–C to the $17\frac{1}{2}'' \times 20\frac{1}{2}''$ dark blue multicolored-speckle print block.

2. Refer to Finishing Your Quilt (pages 70–73) to layer, baste, and quilt your quilt. Use the $1\frac{1}{4}''$ medium pink print strips for binding.

3. Refer to the quilt photo and the detail photo below. Stitch a single strand (or multiple strands, if you prefer) of white yarn through all layers of the quilt, and then knot securely to make the kitty's whiskers. Repeat using the pink yarn or embroidery floss to make random knots on the kitty for fur.

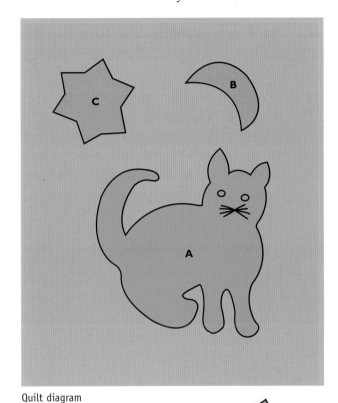

Quilt diagram

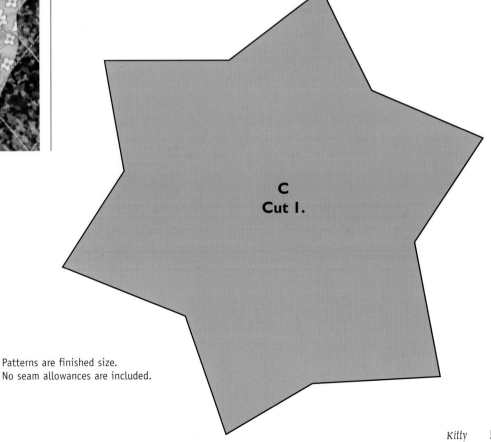

C
Cut 1.

Patterns are finished size.
No seam allowances are included.

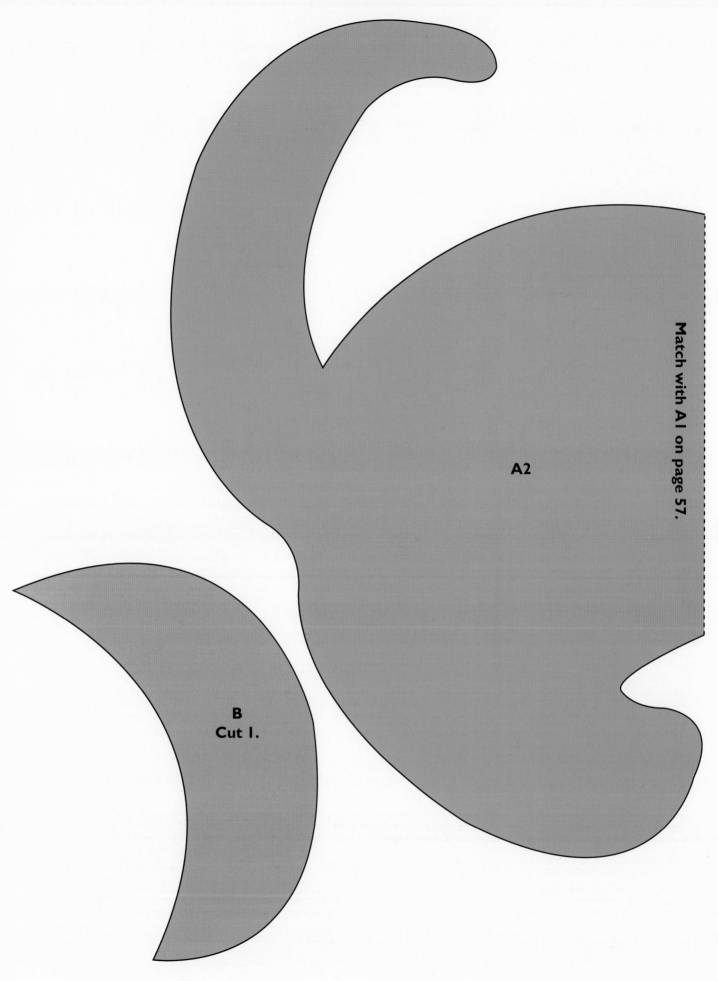

A2

Match with A1 on page 57.

B
Cut 1.

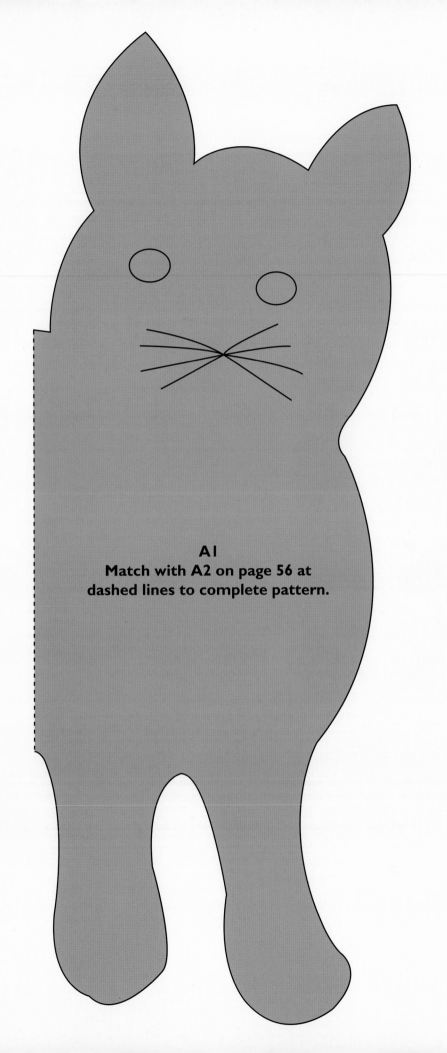

A1
Match with A2 on page 56 at
dashed lines to complete pattern.

Plaid Baskets

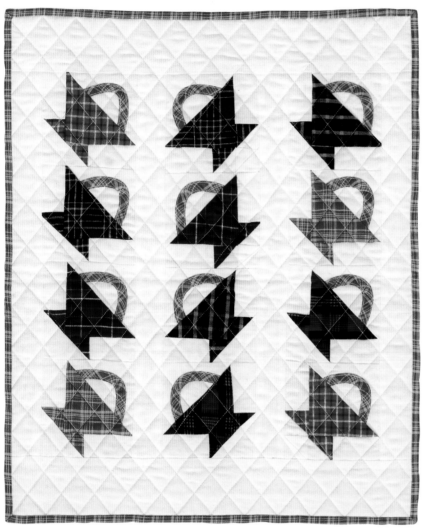

Plaid Baskets, 17¼″ × 19½″, designed and made by Gwen Marston, 1999. The woven look of plaids makes them a great choice for scrappy basket quilts.

Materials

Yardages are based on fabric that measures 40″ wide after laundering.

- ⅔ yard muslin for block background, sashing strips, and borders
- Fat eighth (9″ × 21″) *each* of 6 assorted homespuns for baskets
- ⅔ yard rust homespun for basket handles and binding*
- ⅔ yard fabric for backing
- 22″ × 24″ piece of batting

*May be one of the assorted homespuns.

Cutting

Cut strips across the fabric width (selvage to selvage).

From the muslin:

Cut 1 strip 3⅝″ × 40″; subcut into 6 squares 3⅝″ × 3⅝″. Cut each square diagonally in 1 direction to make 2 half-square triangles (A) (12 total).

Cut 2 strips 1½″ × 40″; subcut into 24 pieces 1½″ × 2¼″ (C).

Cut 1 strip 2⅝″ × 40″; subcut into 6 squares 2⅝″ × 2⅝″. Cut each square diagonally in 1 direction to make 2 half-square triangles (D) (12 total).

Cut 2 strips 1¾″ × 15½″.

Cut 2 strips 2″ × 15½″.

Cut 1 strip 2½″ × 17¼″.

Cut 1 strip 2¾″ × 17¼″.

From *each* of the 6 assorted homespuns:

Cut 1 square $3\frac{5}{8}$″ × $3\frac{5}{8}$″. Cut the square diagonally in 1 direction to make 2 half-square triangles (A) (12 total).

Cut 2 squares $1\frac{3}{4}$″ × $1\frac{3}{4}$″. Cut each square diagonally in 1 direction to make 2 half-square triangles (B) (24 total).

From the rust homespun:

Cut 1″-wide strips from the bias of the fabric. You will need 48″ of bias for the basket handles.

Cut 3 strips $1\frac{1}{4}$″ × 40″.

Making the Blocks

Note: Use $\frac{1}{4}$″-wide seam allowances for piecing.

1. Refer to Making Stems (page 13), and use the 1″-wide rust homespun strips to make 12 bias strips $\frac{3}{8}$″ × 4″.

2. Refer to Appliqué Basics (pages 6–14), the quilt photo (page 58), and the assembly diagram (at far right), and use your preferred method to appliqué a strip from Step 1 to each muslin A triangle.

3. Sew appliquéd triangles from Step 2 and assorted homespun A triangles in pairs as shown. Press. Make 12.

Make 12.

4. Sew an assorted homespun B triangle to each muslin C piece. Press. Make 12 of each in matching sets of 2.

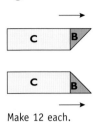

Make 12 each.

5. Sew 1 of each matching-fabric unit from Step 4 to adjacent sides of a matching-fabric unit from Step 3. Press. Make 12.

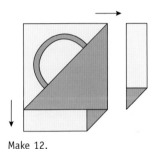

Make 12.

6. Sew a muslin D triangle to each unit from Step 5 as shown. Press. Make 12.

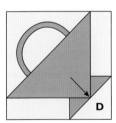

Make 12.

Assembling and Finishing the Quilt

1. Arrange the blocks in 3 vertical rows of 4 blocks each, turning the blocks as shown in the assembly diagram below. Sew the blocks into rows. Press.

2. Arrange and sew the rows from Step 1 and the $1\frac{3}{4}$″ × $15\frac{1}{2}$″ muslin strips, alternating them as shown. Press.

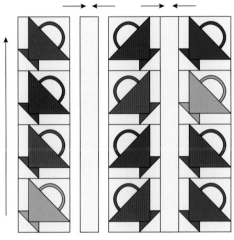

Assembly diagram

3. Refer to Borders (page 71). Sew the 2″ × $15\frac{1}{2}$″ muslin borders to the sides of the quilt. Press. Sew the $2\frac{1}{2}$″ × $17\frac{1}{4}$″ muslin border to the top and the $2\frac{3}{4}$″ × $17\frac{1}{4}$″ border to the bottom. Press.

4. Refer to Finishing Your Quilt (pages 70–73) to layer, baste, and quilt your quilt. Use the $1\frac{1}{4}$″-wide rust homespun strips for binding.

Flower Pot With Bird

Flower Pot With Bird, 18″ × 20″, designed and made by Gwen Marston, 1996. The idea for this old-fashioned-looking quilt came from a circa 1850 quilt shown in Robert Bishop's book *New Discoveries in American Quilts* (see Bibliography on page 79). I'm always looking for new ideas to try, and I was attracted to the unusually wide stems in the older quilt.

Materials

Yardages are based on fabric that measures 40″ wide after laundering.

- ⅔ yard light yellow print for background
- Fat quarter (18″ × 21″) dark green print for stems and leaf (B) and flower cup (D) appliqués
- 8″ × 7″ scrap of dark blue print for vase appliqué (A)
- Fat quarter (18″ × 21″) medium-dark red print for flower appliqués (C, E, F, G, and G reverse)
- 8″ × 6″ scrap of brown print for bird appliqué (H)
- ¼ yard red small-scale print for binding
- ⅔ yard fabric for backing
- 22″ × 24″ piece of batting

Cutting

Cut strips across the fabric width (selvage to selvage) unless otherwise noted. Patterns for appliqué shapes (A–H) appear on pages 61–63.

From the light yellow print:
Cut 1 piece 18½″ × 20½″.

From the dark green print:
Cut 2″-wide strips from the bias of the fabric. You will need 36″ of bias for the stems.
Cut 6 B.
Cut 1 D.

From the dark blue print scrap:
Cut 1 A.

From the medium-dark red print:
    Cut 1 *each* C, E, and F.
    Cut 1 G and 1 G reverse.

From the brown print scrap:
    Cut 1 H.

From the red small-scale print:
    Cut 3 strips 1¼″ × 40″.

Appliquéing and Finishing the Quilt

Refer to Appliqué Basics (pages 6–14), the quilt photo (page 60), and the quilt diagram (at right) as needed for guidance with technique and placement.

1. Refer to Making Stems (page 13), and use the 2″-wide dark green print strips to make a single strip 1″ × 36″.

2. Using the strip from Step 1, trim, place, and appliqué 5 stems to the 18½″ × 20½″ light yellow print block.

3. Use your preferred method to place and appliqué 1 A and 6 B to the block.

4. Place and appliqué 1 each of C and D to the top stem and E, F, G, and G reverse to the ends of the remaining stems.

5. Place and appliqué H to the block.

6. Refer to Finishing Your Quilt (pages 70–73) to layer, baste, and quilt your quilt. Use the 1¼″ red small-scale print strips for binding.

Quilt diagram

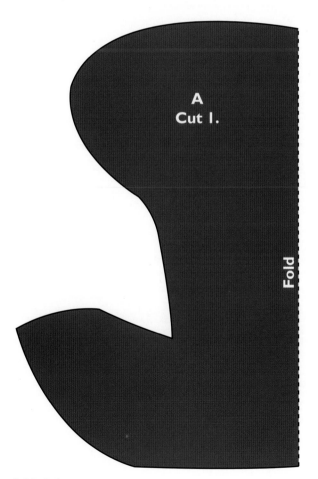

Patterns are finished size.
No seam allowances are included.

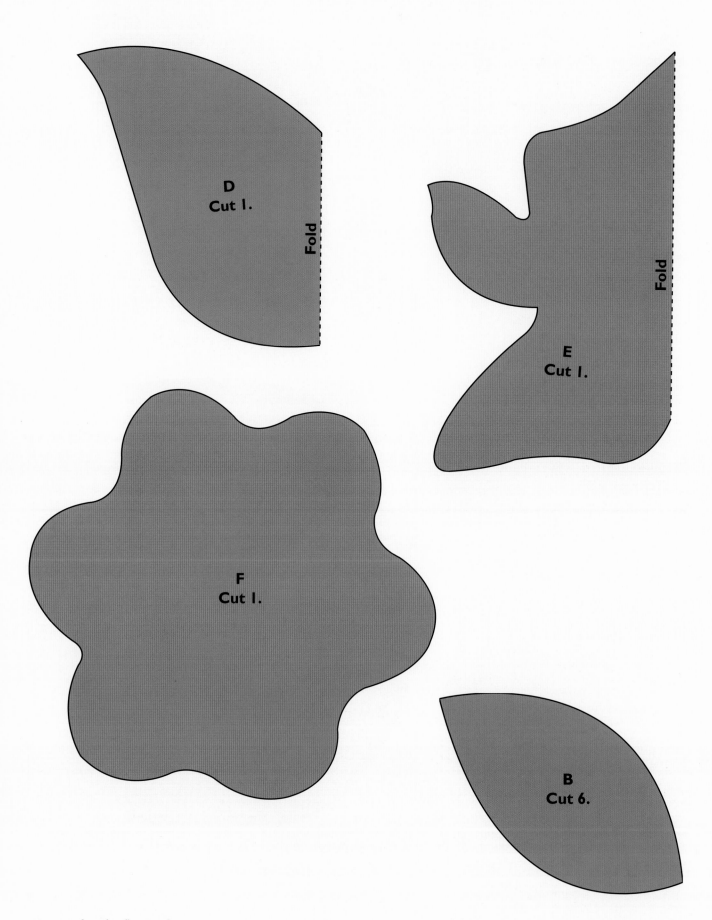

D
Cut 1.

Fold

E
Cut 1.

Fold

F
Cut 1.

B
Cut 6.

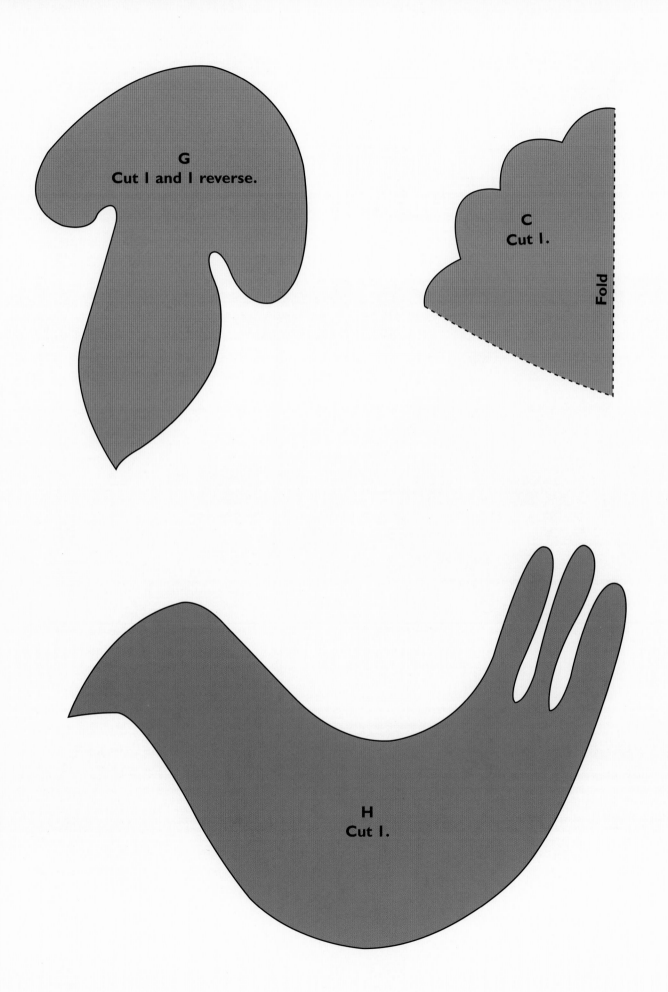

G
Cut 1 and 1 reverse.

C
Cut 1.

Fold

H
Cut 1.

Aunt Anne's South Carolina Lily

Aunt Anne's South Carolina Lily, 18″ × 21″, designed and made by Judy Hester, 1998. Here is a wonderful quilt, made by my late friend Judy Hester and given to me as a gift. Judy made the block, I set it into a quilt, and Judy did the quilting. Judy pieced her quilts by hand and was a masterful hand quilter. This is a beautiful example of her work.

This pattern is traditionally known as North Carolina Lily, but Judy changed the name to South Carolina Lily in honor of her Aunt Anne, whose quilt Judy replicated and who lived in the Palmetto State.

Materials

Yardages are based on fabric that measures 40″ wide after laundering.

- ⅔ yard muslin for block background, sawtooth border, and setting triangles
- ⅛ yard yellow solid for block and sawtooth border
- ¼ yard medium green solid for block, sawtooth border, and top and bottom border
- ⅓ yard red small-scale print for block and binding
- ⅔ yard fabric for backing
- 22″ × 25″ piece of batting

Cutting

Cut strips across the fabric width (selvage to selvage). Pattern for piece A appears on page 66.

From the muslin:

Cut 2 squares 3″ × 3″. Cut each square diagonally in both directions to make 4 quarter-square triangles (C) (8 total). You will have 2 triangles left over.

Cut 3 squares 1¾″ × 1¾″ (D).

Cut 1 square 4⅛″ × 4⅛″. Cut diagonally in 1 direction to make 2 half-square triangles (E).

Cut 1 square 3½″ × 3½″ (F).

Cut 2 strips 1¾″ × 6¾″ (I).

Cut 1 square 3⅜″ × 3⅜″. Cut diagonally in 1 direction to make 2 half-square triangles (J). You will have 1 triangle left over.

Cut 1 strip 2⅛″ × 40″; subcut into 16 squares 2⅛″ × 2⅛″. Cut each square diagonally in 1 direction to make 2 half-square triangles (K) (32 total).

Cut 2 squares 10″ × 10″. Cut each square diagonally in 1 direction to make 2 half-square triangles (L) (4 total).

From the yellow solid:

Cut 12 A.

Cut 1 strip 2⅛″ × 40″; subcut into 14 squares 2⅛″ × 2⅛″. Cut each square diagonally in 1 direction to make 2 half-square triangles (K) (28 total).

From the medium green solid:

Cut 2 squares 2⅝″ × 2⅝″. Cut each square diagonally in 1 direction to make 2 half-square triangles (B) (4 total). You will have 1 triangle left over.

Cut 3 bias strips 1″ × 4″.

Cut 2 squares 2⅛″ × 2⅛″. Cut each square diagonally in 1 direction to make 2 half-square triangles (K) (4 total).

Cut 2 strips 1¾″ × 18″.

From the red small-scale print:

Cut 1 square 5⅜″ × 5⅜″. Cut diagonally in 1 direction to make 2 half-square triangles (G). You will have 1 triangle left over.

Cut 1 square 2⅛″ × 2⅛″. Cut diagonally in 1 direction to make 2 half-square triangles (H).

Cut 3 strips 1¼″ × 40″.

Making the Blocks

Note: Use ¼″-wide seam allowances for piecing.

1. Sew 2 yellow solid A diamonds together as shown. Press. Make

6. Sew 2 units together. Press. Make 3.

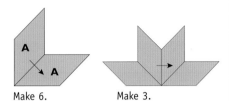

Make 6.   Make 3.

2. Sew a medium green solid B triangle to each unit from Step 1 as shown. Press. Make 3.

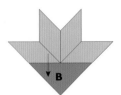

Make 3.

3. Sew 2 muslin C triangles and 1 muslin D square to each unit from Step 2, insetting the triangles and square as shown. Start sewing ¼″ from the raw edges, and sew in the direction of the arrows. Press. Make 1 of each of the 3 variations.

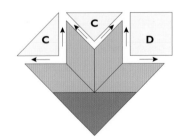

Sew in direction of arrows.

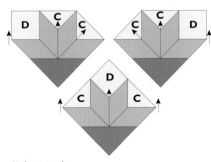

Make 1 each.

4. Sew a muslin E triangle to opposite sides of the appropriate unit from Step 3 as shown. Press.

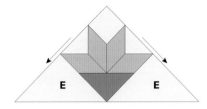

5. Refer to Making Stems (page 13), and use the 1″-wide medium green solid strips to make 3 strips ¼″ × 4″.

6. Refer to Appliqué Basics (pages 6–14), and use your preferred method to appliqué the strips from Step 5 to the muslin F piece as shown.

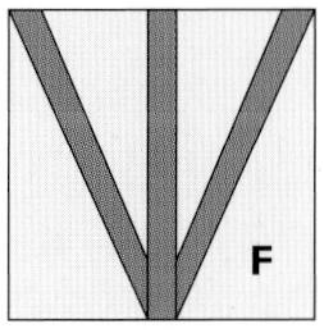

7. Arrange and sew the remaining units from Step 3, the unit from Step 4, the unit from Step 6, and the red small-scale print G triangle together as shown. Press.

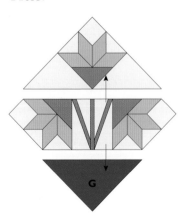

8. Sew a red small-scale print H triangle to each muslin I strip as shown. Press. Make 1 of each. Sew to adjacent sides of the unit from Step 7. Press.

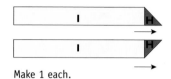

Make 1 each.

9. Sew the muslin J triangle to the unit from Step 8 as shown. Press. Trim the block to 9¼″ × 9¼″.

Making and Adding the Sawtooth Border

1. Sew muslin K triangles and yellow solid K triangles together in pairs. Press. Make 28. Sew muslin K triangles and medium green solid K triangles together in pairs. Press. Make 4.

Make 28.   Make 4.

2. Sew 7 muslin/yellow units from Step 1 together as shown. Press. Make 2.

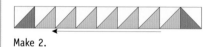

Make 2.

3. Sew 7 muslin/yellow units and 2 muslin/medium green units from Step 1 together as shown. Press. Make 2.

Make 2.

4. Sew a unit from Step 2 to opposite sides of the block. Press. Sew a unit from Step 3 to the remaining sides of the block. Press.

Assembling and Finishing the Quilt

1. Refer to the assembly diagram below. Sew a muslin L triangle to opposite sides of the block. Press. Sew a muslin L triangle to each remaining side. Press. Trim the quilt to 18″ × 18″.

Assembly diagram

2. Refer to Borders (page 71). Sew a 1¾″ × 18″ medium green solid strip to the top and bottom of the quilt. Press.

3. Refer to Finishing Your Quilt (pages 70–73) to layer, baste, and quilt your quilt. Use the 1¼″ red small-scale print strips for binding.

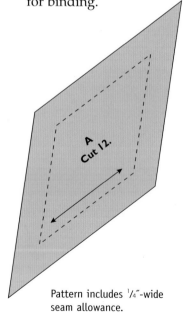

A
Cut 12.

Pattern includes ¼″-wide seam allowance.

Chicken VI: Mama's Got a Brand New 'Do

Chicken VI: Mama's Got a Brand New 'Do, 17″ × 20½″, designed and made by Gwen Marston, 2003. This simple design is made more interesting by the pieced background. The fabric choices all support the theme. Checks say "country," eggs say "chicken," and the print along the bottom edge says—what else?—"chicken tracks"!

Materials

Yardages are based on fabric that measures 40″ wide after laundering.

- ½ yard *total* of 3 small-scale checks for background*
- 3″ × 21″ strip green print for background
- 2 bias strips 1¼″ × 6″ of red print for chicken legs
- Small scrap of black multicolored-polka-dot print for comb appliqué (A)
- Fat quarter (18″ × 21″) black egg print for chicken body appliqué (B)
- Small scrap of bright yellow solid for eye reverse appliqué
- ⅔ yard fabric for backing

I used 2 tan checks—1 light and 1 medium value—and 1 blue check.

Cutting

Cut strips across the fabric width (selvage to selvage). Patterns for appliqué shapes (A and B) appear on pages 68–69.

From the black multicolored-polka-dot print scrap:
    Cut 1 A.

From the black egg print:
    Cut 1 B (B1 and B2).

From the backing fabric:
    Cut 1 piece 17½″ × 21″.

Piecing, Appliquéing, and Finishing the Quilt

Note: Use ¼″-wide seam allowances for piecing.

Refer to Appliqué Basics (pages 6–14), the quilt photo (page 67), and the quilt diagram (below) as needed for guidance with technique and placement.

1. Use the 3 different checks and the 3″ × 21″ green print strip to randomly piece the quilt background. Don't worry about exactly matching my quilt background as shown in the diagram below; just use it for inspiration. When you are satisfied with the results, trim to 17½″ × 21″.

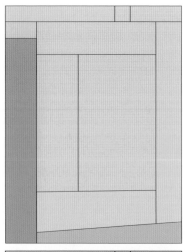

Quilt diagram

2. Refer to Making Stems (page 13), and use the 1¼″-wide red print bias strips to make 2 strips ⅝″ × 6″.

3. Place and appliqué the red print strips from Step 2 to the pieced background block from Step 1 to make chicken legs.

4. Refer to Adding Reverse Appliqué (page 12), and appliqué the bright yellow solid scrap to piece B.

5. Use your preferred method to place and appliqué 1 each of A and B to the block.

6. Layer the quilt top and the 17½″ × 21″ piece of backing fabric right sides together, carefully aligning the raw edges. Pin. Sew around the outside edges using a ¼″-wide seam. Leave a 4″ opening for turning.

7. Turn the quilt right side out, and hand stitch the opening closed.

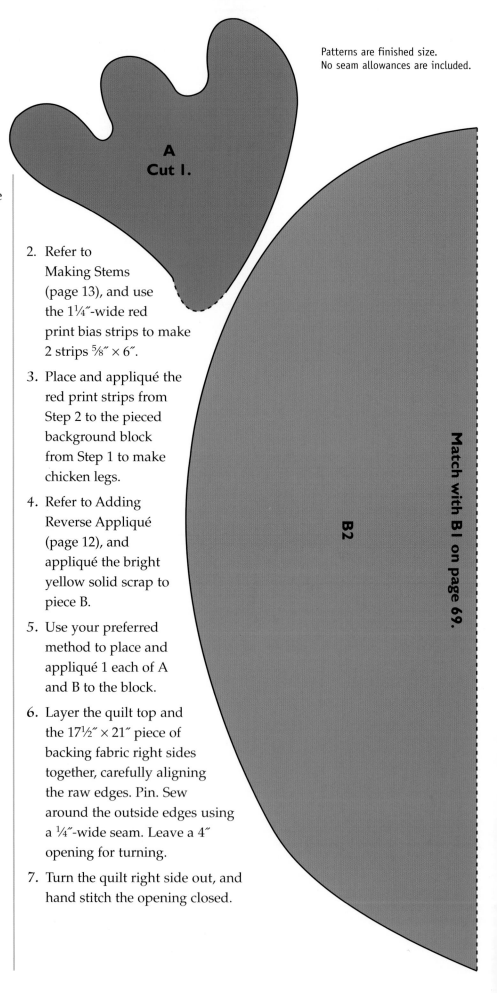

Patterns are finished size.
No seam allowances are included.

A
Cut 1.

B2

Match with B1 on page 69.

B1
Match with B2 on page 68 at
dashed lines to complete pattern.

Finishing Your Quilt

The following information will help you to add borders and to transform
the quilt top you have made into a wonderful finished quilt.

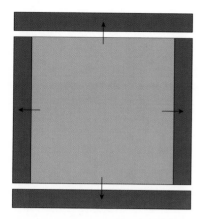

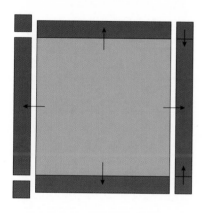

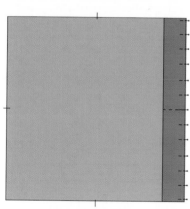

Borders

The first thing about borders is that you don't have to have them. (You'll notice that many of the small quilts in this book have no borders.) If you opt for the no-border approach, you don't need to read any further in this section. If you do choose to add a border to your quilt, read on.

I like to postpone design decisions about borders until the interior of the quilt is done. My feeling is that I can make better choices at that point because I have the completed body of the quilt to look at. I lay the quilt on the floor and start toying with different possibilities.

I seldom use mitered corners on borders, as they were rarely used before 1970. Instead, I use butt joints for the corners on my quilts. I add the side borders first and then sew on the top and bottom borders.

Sometimes I make borders with corner squares or units. I add the top and bottom borders, join the corner squares or units to the side borders, and then sew the side borders to the quilt.

It is worth taking your time and working carefully when adding the borders to your quilt. Here is the method I use:

1. Press the quilt top so it lies as flat as possible. Spread the quilt on the floor or on another flat surface.

2. Measure the quilt down the center, from top to bottom and from side to side. I think this method gives the most accurate measurement. I also measure all four sides of the quilt.

My goal is to cut the borders the exact size they should be, based on my measurements through the centers. Then I make the body of the quilt fit the border. Lay the border along the edge of the quilt. Match and pin the two ends. Pin the quilt and the border together at the midpoint, and then keep dividing the halves into smaller halves, pinning generously.

Backing

Cut your backing approximately 4″ larger in both directions than your finished quilt top. The quilts in this book are small enough that you will not need to piece the backing. You may, however, do so if that is your choice. There are no rules: choose the way that is most practical or that suits your personal taste.

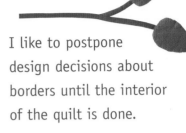

Batting

I prefer to use 100% cotton batting in my quilts because I like the look of antique quilts, and I like natural fibers. Others prefer polyester batting because of its loft and because it is easier to needle and doesn't need to be quilted as closely as cotton.

I cut the batting by layering it over the stretched backing, smoothing it out, and trimming the excess. This method requires no measuring.

I like to postpone design decisions about borders until the interior of the quilt is done.

Layering and Basting

Most of today's quilters quilt in a hoop or portable frame that requires basting. Here is one method to use for layering and basting your quilt.

Press the backing and the quilt top, clipping any stray threads. Spread the backing right side down on a clean, flat surface. Secure the edges with masking tape or T-pins. Center and smooth the batting, and then the quilt top, right side up over the backing.

If you plan to hand quilt, baste the layers together with a long needle and light-colored thread. Baste the vertical and horizontal centerlines first, and then baste in a grid with lines of stitches no more than 3″ to 4″ apart. Finish by basting around the entire perimeter of the quilt top.

If you plan to machine quilt, follow the same process, substituting small, rustproof safety pins for the needle and thread.

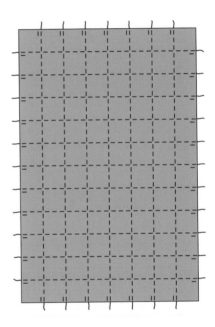

Quilting

As in every other design phase, when choosing the quilting designs for my little quilts, I look to antique quilts for guidance. I often outline the appliqué shapes and fill in the backgrounds with crosshatched grids or other linear fill designs. I also enjoy adapting feather, leaf, plume, and floral motifs from old quilts, often drawing them freehand.

Binding

The majority of nineteenth-century quilts were bound with a single-fold binding cut on the straight of the goods. This is my preferred method, as well. A single-fold binding is easy to handle and gives your quilt a fine finished edge. The double-fold binding so popular today seems too bulky for my taste, particularly for little quilts.

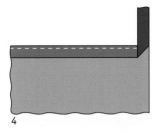

4

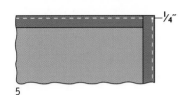

5

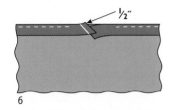

6

7

8

1. Carefully trim the batting and backing even with the edge of the quilt top on all sides.

2. Use a rotary cutter and a sturdy ruler to cut the necessary number of strips 1¼″ wide. Join the strips with a diagonal seam, as shown on page 13; this method helps the finished seam lie flat.

3. Align the binding with the raw edge of the quilt top, right sides together. Leaving the first few inches of binding unsewn, stitch the binding to the quilt with a ¼″-wide seam.

4. To miter the corners, sew to exactly ¼″ from the corner of the quilt. Backstitch, lift the presser foot, and pull the quilt away from the sewing machine. Fold the binding up and away from the quilt at a 45° angle as shown.

5. Fold the binding down, and carefully resume stitching with a ¼″-wide seam exactly ¼″ from the corner as shown. Continue in this manner until you have turned the final corner.

6. Stop sewing about 5″ from the place where you began attaching the binding to the quilt. Remove the quilt from the sewing machine. Place both ends of the binding along the edge of the quilt and overlap the ends. Draw a pencil line at a 45° angle along the edge of the binding strip on top. Trim the strip ½″ past the drawn line.

7. Join the ends of the binding with a ¼″-wide seam. Finger-press the seam open. Finish stitching the binding to the quilt.

8. Bring the binding to the back of the quilt, fold the raw edge of the binding under, and hand stitch the binding in place with thread that matches the quilt's outermost border. This keeps the stitches invisible in case you inadvertently stitch through to the quilt top.

Gallery

Leopard, 18″ × 20″, designed and made by Gwen Marston, 1999. Hand quilted by Valerie Clarke. The shape of the leopard was inspired by an African panel made in Ghana by the Fante, a people with a long history of making appliqué banners to pass along traditional wisdom aimed at making everyday life easier.

The panel that inspired my quilt showed a man lying on the ground with a leopard standing on his chest. The lesson to consider: if you shoot a leopard and do not kill the leopard, it would been better not to have shot the leopard at all. These are words to live by!

Two Birds With Cherries, 18″ × 20″, designed and made by Gwen Marston, 1995. When I need a new shape for a vase, I look at all my books picturing antique quilts. That's where I found the inspiration for the vase in this quilt, which has always reminded me of a dog dish with antlers. Sometimes I refer to it affectionately as the "Bullwinkle vase," after the well-known cartoon moose.

My Pink Tulips, 18″ × 20″, designed and made by Gwen Marston, 1994. In the spring of 1994, my garden featured an impressive crop of bright pink tulips, which I decided to capture in this quilt. Unfortunately, the tulips also made a big impression on the deer in the neighborhood, so only this dear little quilt remains.

Feed Sack Shoo Fly, 14″ × 19¼″, designed and made by Gwen Marston, 1995. This classic country design works beautifully with feed sack fabrics. Although I used vintage feed sacks from the early twentieth century, you can easily substitute the wonderful 1930s reproduction prints widely available today.

Chicken XIII, 15¹/₂″ × 18″, designed and made by Gwen Marston, 2003. This quilt is another example of fabric choices that help deliver the message. The message this quilt relays is simple and to the point: CHICKEN.

Five Red Tulips, 18″ × 20″, designed and made by Gwen Marston, 2001. These whimsical red tulips repeat themselves simply in a wide spray. A bit of embroidery, including stem stitch and French knots worked in lavender thread, adds a nice touch. This composition reminds us that uncomplicated arrangements can also be pleasing and that clean, uncluttered design can be refreshing.

Gwen's Baskets, 17½″ × 19″, designed and made by Gwen Marston, 2001. Machine quilted by Sue Nickels. This quilt is a simplified version of an antique basket quilt. I've never seen another basket pattern exactly like this one.

Flower Pot and Sawtooth, 17½″ × 19″, designed and made by Gwen Marston, 1993. My favorite sawtooth border sets off this basket of flowers. Of all the pieced sawtooth variations, this one seems the liveliest.

About the Author

Gwen Marston is a quiltmaker who has had many exhibits in the United States and one in Japan. She learned to make quilts from a group of Mennonite women and still uses traditional methods to create her work. She lectures and teaches quiltmaking around the country and has hosted quilt retreats in northern Michigan for the past 23 years. She has written 21 books, including *Liberated String Quilts* (C&T Publishing, 2003) and *Classic Four-Block Appliqué Quilts* (C&T Publishing, 2005). She also designs a line of patterns—The Gwen Marston Collection—for JWD Publishing.

Other C&T books by Gwen Marston:

Bibliography

Adler, Peter, and Nicholas Barnard. *Asafo: African Flags of the Fante*. London: Thames and Hudson, 1992.

Bishop, Robert. *New Discoveries in American Quilts*. New York: E.P. Dutton, 1975.

Cross, Mary Bywater. *Treasures in the Trunk: Quilts of the Oregon Trail*. Nashville, TN: Rutledge Hill Press, 1993.

Fox, Sandi. *Small Endearments: 19th-Century Quilts for Children*. New York: Charles Scribner's Sons, 1985.

Kimball, Jeana. *Red and Green: An Appliqué Tradition*. Bothell, WA: That Patchwork Place, 1990.

Kiracofe, Roderick. *The American Quilt*. New York: Clarkson Potter, 1993.

Marston, Gwen. *Classic Four-Block Appliqué Quilts*. Lafayette, CA: C&T Publishing, 2005.

_____. *Mary Schafer, American Quilt Maker*. Ann Arbor: University of Michigan Press, 2004.

_____. *Twenty Little Amish Quilts*. New York: Dover Publications, 1993.

_____. *Twenty Little Four-Patch Quilts*. New York: Dover Publications, 1996.

_____. *Twenty Little Log Cabin Quilts*. New York: Dover Publications, 1995.

_____. *Twenty Little Pinwheel Quilts*. New York: Dover Publications, 1994.

_____. *Twenty Little Triangle Quilts*. New York: Dover Publications, 1997.

Marston, Gwen, and Joe Cunningham. *Twenty Little Patchwork Quilts*. New York: Dover Publications, 1990.

Pellman, Rachel, and Kenneth Pellman. *Amish Doll Quilts, Dolls, and Other Playthings*. Intercourse, PA: Good Books, 1986.

Woodward, Thomas K., and Blanche Greenstein. *Crib Quilts and Other Small Wonders*. New York: E.P. Dutton, 1981.

For a free catalog of C&T Publishing books and products:
C&T Publishing, Inc.
Box 1456
Lafayette, CA 94549
(800) 284-1114
ctinfo@ctpub.com
www.ctpub.com

To order Gwen's patterns:
JWD Publishing
104 Bon Bluff
Fox Island, WA 98333
(253) 549-7889
dwolfrom@jwdpublishing.com
www.jwdpublishing.com

For quilting supplies:
Cotton Patch Mail Order
3405 Hall Lane, Dept. CTB
Lafayette, CA 94549
(800) 835-4418
(925) 283-7883
quiltusa@yahoo.com
www.quiltusa.com

Note: Fabric manufacturers discontinue fabrics regularly. Exact fabrics shown may no longer be available.

Great Titles from 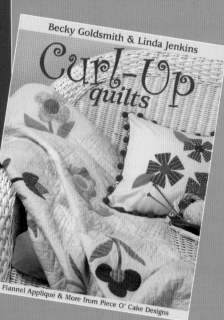 C&T PUBLISHING

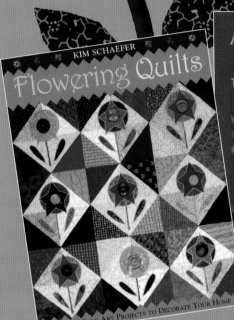

Available at your local retailer or
www.ctpub.com or 800.284.1114